Starting your own
Dog Home Boarding Business

Tamsin Stone

Published By T-Squared

ISBN 978-0-9543500-3-1

British Library Cataloguing in Publication Data
A catalogue record for this book is available in the British Library

Published by T- Squared,
Bedfordshire

Although every effort has been made to ensure that the information in this book was correct at press time, neither the author or publisher assumes any liability resulting from action taken based on the information included herein. Laws and regulations are complex and subject to change, and readers should check the current position with relevant authorities or obtain appropriate legal, financial or other professional advice before making personal arrangements. Mention of a company name does not constitute endorsement.

Contents

Acknowledgements

Thank you to the following boarders for sharing their experience:

Carole Morgan, Chez Jasper
Hayley Elliott-Edwards, Scruffy Mutts
Katherine White, Happy Pawz home dog boarding
Linda Derosa, Dinky Dogz Home Boarding
Claire Harper, Your Pet Pal
Lisa Clark, Birtle Home Boarding
Penny Wight, Penelope Petstop
Steph Drake, Total Pet Expert
Kim Knowles, Bertie & Shelby's Home from Home Holiday
Hayley Corbett, Hayleysbowwows
Janie Wellman, The Wellmans Dog Home Boarding
Alice Paton, Alice's Home Boarding for Dogs
Beccy Harris, Doggy Paws Indoors
Bev Halstead, Ffoslas Farm Pet Hotel
Debbie Humphreys, Debbieduz Home Dog Boarding
Liz Knights, Oaklands Home Boarding
Mathew Godwin
Alice Paton, Alice's Home Boarding for Dogs
Lyndsay Moon, Happy Doggy Daycare

1

Starting a Dog Home Boarding Business

In recent years, dogs have enjoyed a raise in status from family pet to family member, and business for retailers catering to their needs is booming. We spend over £5 billion a year on high tech toys, luxury treats, gourmet food and grooming boutiques. Pet owners are demanding more when it comes to holiday care too; they want a boarding provider who will give their dog the same loving care and comfortable surroundings they receive at home.

This has led to the development of the dog home boarding industry, where dogs stay in private homes living as a family pet rather than in the concrete pens of a traditional boarding kennel. Dogs staying with a home boarder go for regular walks, play in private gardens and snuggle up on the sofa or in front of the fire in the evening. This home-from-home style care is a growing market and dog owners are willing to pay a premium for a friendly professional service.

For those who enjoy the company of dogs, starting a home boarding service might seem like the perfect job – being paid to do something you'd happily do for free. There is much more to running a boarding business than cuddling puppies though. Dog boarders are subject to a range of laws and regulations, need licences and insurance, have to pay tax and National Insurance, and have to meet the high expectations pet owners have of professional dog carers.

For the last ten years I've run a boarding directory helping pet boarders market their services. During this time I've seen many boarding business thrive, providing a service that caters to dogs' needs and giving the boarder a rewarding and profitable career, but I've also seen many start-ups fail. The problem is almost always that the beginner boarder didn't do enough research or plan their service as a business; they just popped up an advert and hoped to take bookings. To help make sure you're one of the success stories, this guide aims to walk you through the process of setting up and running a successful boarding business and avoid the potential pitfalls along the way.

Is Dog Boarding the Business for You?

Before we jump into starting your business, it's a good idea to pause and double check that your expectations of being a home boarding provider match up with the realities. In other words, is this business really the one for you?

Legal requirements

Anyone running a dog boarding business in the UK must apply for a licence. To be granted a licence you need have your home inspected and comply with a range of conditions that will place restrictions on how you run your business. There are also a range of other laws that apply to people caring for dogs or running a small business from home. You'll need to comply with animal welfare legislation, consumer business law, register as self-employed, keep records of your income and expenses, and submit an annual tax return.

Skills and experience

Enjoying the company of dogs is a prerequisite for running a boarding business, but providing a professional service is not the same as looking after your own pet. You'll need to understand diet and welfare requirements, be knowledgeable and experienced at managing a wide range of dog behaviour issues, and be able to cope with any health problems that arise. You need to be willing to follow directions, within reason, from dog owners whose ideas about dog care may be different from yours. Previous experience working with different breeds, personalities and levels of training will be very helpful. You'll also need to have or develop skills unrelated to dogs, including marketing, accounting and customer services.

Working with people

If you are choosing boarding because you prefer to work with animals over people, you may be disappointed. Boarders have to deal with dog owners, not just their dogs – you'll have to answer calls, negotiate with clients, meet nervous dog owners and may even be asked to provide advice on dog care. Many clients will be lovely and you'll form long-term relationships with them and their dogs, but some clients may be more difficult to work with, and you may not always be able to afford the luxury of picking and choosing.

Hard work and responsibility

As a home boarder you'll be working a twenty-four hour day, and be responsible for feeding, walking, and making sure the dog is safe and seeking veterinary attention when necessary. If a dog becomes ill at 3am you'll be the one off to the emergency vet.

Dogs may require two or three long walks every day; that's a lot of miles to cover so you'll need to be fit and active. On a sunny afternoon a walk with dogs can seem the perfect way to spend your time, but you'll also be walking through rain, wind and sometimes snow and will have muddy wet dogs to clean up afterwards.

There is no holiday pay or sick leave, and you'll need to be in a fit state to supervise dogs (or drive to the vets) at all times.

Stress

Running your own business, even one that involves cuddling puppies, can be stressful. If you have a problem, there is no colleague or boss to turn to; you have to resolve it yourself. You need to be a responsible person who can plan their own day and stick to it without someone chivvying them along. You'll also need to be able to deal with criticism, and be willing to honestly assess your own performance and business so you can make improvements.

 What's running a boarding service really like?

"Boarding is most rewarding - such a lovely job, looking after people's beloved fur babies. However it's not a money-spinner!"

- Carole Morgan, Chez Jasper

"Everyone thinks it's an easy job, it really isn't! It can be stressful, tiring and hard work but equally it can be lovely and rewarding too. The worst part is your house never being just yours. My little boy can't have his train set scattered around the living room and he can't run through the house like a loon as he has to be mindful of boarding dogs. It's not a 9-5 job it's 24/7. You can't just go out to a party or take the kids out for the day."

- Hayley Elliott-Edwards, Scruffy Mutts

"I love boarding. The dogs are the best part, I love getting to know each character. The hard part is the regular dogs become part of the family and when they pass away or become ill it's just as heartbreaking for me as the owners."

- Katherine White, Happy Pawz home dog boarding

Family life

If you share your home with other people you'll need to think about the impact boarding dogs will have on them. Even if you plan to be doing all the work, you can't board dogs in your family home without expecting it to have some impact on your family. Before you commit to becoming a home boarder you need to make sure that anyone who lives with you is happy with your plans.

Although home boarding might seem like a good choice for a flexible job where you can be at home with your family, it still means you have commitments. You can't put off walking a dog because your child is home from school sick; you are being paid to provide a service and you need to ensure you can do so. There is a time limit on how long you can leave dogs alone, and for dogs with separation anxiety this limit may be zero. That means you can't pop out to see a school play or go for a meal out unless it's practical to take the dogs with you.

But, it can be a great job

It's not all doom and gloom. Yes you'll need to jump through some hoops to set up, work hard and fill in a lot of paperwork, but in return you can have a career that is very rewarding.

You will be your own boss and be able to set your hours and business terms. You can spend a lot of time playing with dogs and learning about dog care and behaviour; the experience you build up could be useful in other dog-related fields such as training or behaviour counselling. You'll have an active lifestyle, with no sitting in an office all day. It could be the perfect job for you.

How much will you earn?

Although caring for dogs can be fun and for many people is a dream job, for most it also needs to be a profitable business that provides enough income to support your lifestyle. You need to be realistic about your potential income, how likely you are to reach that total and whether that will be enough for your needs.

You may have multiplied the daily rate you expect to be paid for boarding by two or three dogs and come up with a tempting sounding total for a year's work. In reality your income is likely to be lower than this. To get a better idea of your actual earning potential you need to factor in the following:

- Your business is unlikely to be an instant success; it will take time for you to build up your customer base to a level where you are regularly operating at full capacity. This means your first year of trading is likely to generate a lower income than later years and you'll need to be able to financially survive this period.

- Boarding is a seasonal business; although people use boarders all year round, you'll be most busy at peak holiday periods. Unlike regular employment where you'll generally receive a similar wage each month, your monthly income is likely to go up and down across the year.
- Bookings don't always neatly slot together, you may have a dog booked for a long weekend that goes home Tuesday, and then a gap until Friday when another dog arrives for a week's holiday.
- Being self-employed means no paid holidays or sick leave – any time off or holidays you have will reduce your income.
- Demand for your services will influence the number of bookings and how much you can charge. If there is a surfeit of boarders in your area, prices will be lower and you'll have to work harder to gain customers.
- You need to account for expenses such as your boarding licence, insurance, any changes necessary to make your home meet the licence conditions, wear and tear on your furniture and decor, car expenses if you transport dogs and equipment you use, such as poop bags. These all need to be deducted from your income before you calculate your profit.
- Any income you make is subject to tax and National Insurance, which you'll need to pay to HMRC. To compare what you'll make boarding with your take-home pay from employment (where your wage is paid after tax) you'll need to deduct the tax you will be paying.

You'll find more about calculating income on page 90.

Restrictions on Using Your Home as a Business

Now you've established if dog boarding could be the job for you, there are a few final hurdles to consider that may affect your ability to run a boarding business from your home.

Suitability of your property

There are few specific rules about the furnishing of properties but in general you'll need to have enough room inside to comfortably house dogs; a small property may limit the size and number of dogs you are licensed to board. If you plan to board more than one dog or have a dog of your own you'll need space to separate them if necessary. Outside space (private not communal) is usually a requirement of a boarding licence although there is no set amount you need. Your home's entrance should also be private and not through a shared/communal entrance.

Planning permission

Normally you don't need planning permission to board a limited number of dogs in your own home, as you are not changing the use from 'mainly a private residence' to a business premises. However, this can change if the council receives complaints that your business activities are causing a nuisance such as noise or odour problems. To prevent this being an issue, you should have a plan for how you'll dispose of waste and deal with barking dogs.

You may need planning permission if you want to make changes to your home such as building an extra room, erecting outbuildings or putting up fencing higher than standard residential. It's unlikely this will apply to someone operating as a home boarder though; if you house dogs in separate accommodation you will need to apply as a boarding kennel.

Tenancy agreement / lease

If your property is rented you need to check whether your tenancy agreement allows you to have dogs and run a business from your home. If it's prohibited, you will need to negotiate with your landlord for permission. Sometimes it helps to offer a higher damage deposit to allay concerns they may have about the impact your work may have on the condition of the property. You could also reassure them that you'll be obtaining insurance cover.

Some tenancy agreements also limit the number of animals that are kept on the property (this would include dogs that are boarding clients), so check carefully for any clauses that could affect your work.

If your landlord finds out that you are breaching your tenancy agreement they may evict you so don't be tempted to try and sneak under their radar.

Mortgage company

Most mortgage companies won't object to you running a business from your home as long as it remains residential (see Planning permission). It's a good idea to double check your mortgage terms just to make sure though.

Restrictive covenants

Some houses have restrictive covenants in the deeds. These prohibit certain activities, such as parking a van on your drive or running a business from the property. This can be a complicated issue, and in older properties covenants may no longer be enforceable. However, they can apply on new estates too and the neighbours and estate management may be more active about enforcing them. If you have a clause that prohibits running a business, a solicitor can offer advice. You can also obtain indemnity insurance policies to protect you if decide to run a business and someone tries to enforce the covenant at a later date.

Children under 5

Most boarding licence conditions forbid boarding in homes with children under the age of five. You'll need to check the exact terms for your area, but even if it's permitted you'll need to consider carefully the risks involved with having dogs, particularly ones you don't know well, interacting with young children.

Franchises and Host Families

This guide is aimed at people intending to start their own independent boarding business, but there are other ways to become a home boarding provider. You can work with another company as a 'host' or you can buy a franchise. Here is a quick overview of these in case it's something you want to investigate further.

Becoming a host family

Host families work for companies that manage networks of different boarders to provide spaces for dogs that are booked. They'll handle the marketing, bookings and payments and you care for the dogs. If starting a business completely from scratch sounds a little daunting or you aren't sure if dog boarding is something you want to do long term then becoming a carer or 'host family' for another boarding company might be a good option for you.

The benefits of this are:

- The marketing is all done for you, and as a larger company they have the budget and established brand recognition so you don't have to build your own.
- Your start-up costs may be lower. Check what you'll have to pay for yourself; for example, they may provide insurance but you may have to pay for your own licence – although they'll usually support you through the process of applying for one.
- You'll have backup. Got a question? They'll be on the line to answer it. Have a problem dog? They can help and even find alternative accommodation if you decide you can't provide care.
- You don't have to board full time, you can just take bookings when you are free. For example, you could take bookings only for weekends and the few weeks a year you are on holiday from your regular employment.

- They'll usually handle all the bookings, payments and billings so you'll have much less paperwork and what you do have they'll usually provide forms for.

The downside is:

- They'll take a portion of the booking cost and you won't be able to set your own rates, so you will probably earn less than doing everything yourself.
- Generally you won't be able to take bookings outside the contract. If you are recommended by someone you'll have to process the booking through them.
- You'll have to abide by their policies on how to run a boarding service (although you'll have final say to turn down a dog for boarding).

Buying a franchise

Some of the companies that manage networks of host families operate as franchises. The parent company sells franchises to people to operate in a specific region, who then recruit and manage all of the host families in that area. A franchise is a licence to operate your business under the brand's name – many restaurants are run this way. Some franchise owners just manage other home boarders, whereas some do some boarding work themselves too.

Pet care franchises cost around £10–15,000 upfront, which gives you the licence to use their brand and usually includes things like a business plan, operating manual with policies on how to run the business, bookkeeping and booking systems, forms, branding such as car signage or clothing with logos, advertising materials such as leaflets, business cards or a website, training and ongoing support.

The benefit of a franchise is they have an established system for running the business, a recognised brand and offer training and support. As you are operating on a larger scale managing many boarders and taking a cut from the bookings you have a higher income potential. The franchise company should be able to give you estimates for outgoings and income based on other franchises in their brand. Make sure you understand the terms they use. For example, 'turnover' refers to the total amount of money taken before expenses, whereas 'profit' is the amount you could actually take as income. Buying a franchise does place some limits on how you can run your business. The goal is to offer a consistent service under a recognised brand so you will have to operate in line with the franchise's rules.

There are numerous franchises operating in the UK and each offer slightly different packages. If it's something you are considering, compare what they offer carefully and speak to the owners to get a better feel for how they are run. If possible speak to existing franchises operating under the brand so you can see how well they follow up on their promises.

Of course, there is no reason why you couldn't start a network of boarders without buying a franchise. That might be something you'd like to think about as a long-term goal for expanding your business.

Writing a Business Plan

Throughout this guide we'll discuss some of the considerations and steps involved in setting up a dog home boarding business. At this point you might consider writing a business plan to organise all this information and make decisions about how you will run your business.

A business plan sets out on paper how you will make your business a success. It encourages you to think about the services you will offer, how you will market yourself (get customers) and to plan your finances (e.g. what you'll charge and what expenses you need to budget for).

A business plan can really help you to think about all the details of how your business will work. It's also a good way to minimise the risk of problems arising from a lack of planning, such as unexpected costs. A business plan is also useful if you need to explain your business to other people – for example, if you are applying for funding or are working with a partner and want to make sure you are on the same page.

If writing a business plan sounds a little bit daunting, don't worry. To make it simple you'll find worksheets throughout this guide that will help you write a business plan or just to think about the decisions you need to make.

Executive summary

The executive summary is the first section of your business plan, but you should write it last, so you're not trying to summarise information you haven't written yet. It acts like a cover letter providing a brief overview of the information in the rest of your business plan, and should include the following:

- Business name
- Tag line (optional)
- Owners name(s)
- Postal address
- Phone number
- Email / Website address

- Legal requirements
- Business summary
- Market summary
- Financial summary
- Business goals
- Date you plan to open

Your business summary should summarise the section about your business describing what service you are going to offer and to whom, what makes you stand out and how you will structure your business. For example:

> *Mel's Dog Home Boarding is a new business run by a qualified pet behaviourist with ten years' experience. It offers dog owners in the middle-income bracket a luxury home-from-home alternative to kennels when they go away on holiday and need pet care. The service is based in the South Bucks area and will cater to owners and their pets living within a 10-mile radius. Dogs will stay in a family home, with exercise and diet requirements tailored to their needs.*

Your market and financial summary should just be a short summary of the relevant sections of your business plan.

Finally, your business goals set out what you want to achieve with your business plan; they need to be specific. You should have a clear test for whether you've achieved what you want and have a time scale. For example "I want to run a successful business" isn't a helpful goal, because you haven't defined what successful is – is it a certain number of bookings, a level of income, or a good balance of work and free time? You also haven't given a timescale for achieving your goal – will you be happy if you become successful in six months or five years? Better goals would be "In one year's time I will be earning a minimum of £600 per month" or "within the first month I will get three new clients". You've defined exactly what you want to achieve and when.

Your goals don't have to be financial, you may prioritise your work-life balance, learning new skills or developing new services. Once you have decided on clear goals, you can plan for how you will achieve them. That might involve things that you'll do or learn to help you get closer to your objective. For example, if your objective is to have your boarding service set up within eight weeks, your plan might include steps and timescales that you'll need to achieve this.

Include some short-term goals (where do you want to be in a year?) and long-term goals (what do you want to achieve in five years?). You'll need to review your goals and your business plan, and update them over time to set new goals as you achieve old ones.

About your business

This section of your plan is all about your proposals for what your business will offer to clients. Think of it like explaining to someone who has never heard of dog boarding what you will do and how your business will work. This section of your business plan should answer the following questions:

- What is your business idea?
- What services will you offer e.g. overnight care, day care, dog walking?
- What are your unique selling points?
- Are there are legal requirements you need to comply with?
- What facilities will you offer and do you need to make changes to your home?
- What geographical area will you target?
- What is your pricing structure?

About you

You are your business's most important asset, so your business plan needs to include a section all about you. This should identify any current skills or experience that will help you in running the business, but also any areas you might need to develop further. For example, you may want to attend a dog first-aid course or read a book on marketing to help widen your knowledge in these areas. Remember this is about running a business, not just caring for dogs, so business-related skills such as accounts or customer service are relevant too. The section about you should answer the following questions:

- What relevant qualifications do you have?
- Do you plan to take any new qualifications and, if so, when?
- What relevant experience do you have in caring for dogs or running a business?
- What are your key skills?
- What do you consider your strengths and weaknesses to be?

Market research

Market research involves finding out about your potential clients and your competitors. The information you gather will influence several areas of your business including your pricing, the services you decide to offer and your advertising. After your market research you should be able to do the following:

- Describe your client base and what they want from a boarding service.
- Have a good idea of the number of potential clients in your area and how much they'll pay for your service.
- Describe your competition including their strengths, weaknesses, prices and marketing.
- Decide where your business will be positioned within the market.
- Explain how your business will stand out from your competitors.

Marketing plan

To gain clients you'll need a plan for how to market your business. In this section you'll list your ideas and how much it will cost to carry them out.

- What techniques will you use to promote your business?
- How much will you budget for promotion?

Financial plan

Before starting your business you need to make sure it's financially viable, that it will generate the income you need for your living expenses. In this section you should show how you've calculated your costs and potential income to prove your business can work financially, including the following:

- Start-up costs and how you will cover them
- Projected income and expenditure
- How much you need to earn to survive e.g. current outgoings
- How many clients you need to achieve the income you projected

To Do List

Now would be a good opportunity to start a list of the steps you need to take to set up your business and a timescale for when you plan complete them. Add to this list as you read this guide to keep track of everything you'll need to do. Once you have made your initial list, you may want to go back and prioritise the order of the items to make sure everything will be completed by your planned launch date.

Items on your list might include the following:

- Discuss your plans with your local council
- Submit an application for a boarding licence
- Choose an insurance provider
- Pisk assess your home and garden for hazards
- Calculate your start-up costs
- Attend a canine first-aid course
- Complete your business plan
- Make a list of equipment you need to buy
- Register as self-employed
- Choose accounting software

2

Legal Requirements

To operate as a home boarder you are legally required to have an animal boarding licence and public liability insurance and comply with legislation regarding the control of dogs and animal welfare. Not complying with these requirements can result in fines or even the loss of your business, so it's important you have a clear understanding of the laws you need to follow.

Animal Boarding Licence

Boarding licences are compulsory for anyone "providing accommodation for other people's dogs in return for payment" including those "working from a private dwelling" not just traditional kennels and catteries. This is set out in the following legislation:

- Animal Boarding Establishments Act 1963 (England, Wales & Scotland)
- Animals Boarding Establishments Regulations (Northern Ireland) 1974.

Obtaining a licence generally involves filling in an application form, paying a fee and having your home inspected. As licences are issued by individual local councils, rather than central government, there is some variation in the process between areas. The information here provides an overview but you'll need to contact your local council to check the specifics for your area.

Licence conditions

Boarding licences have conditions attached which set out the terms under which you must operate. They cover:

- The number of dogs you can board
- Facilities
- Staff training
- Cleanliness

- Food & water
- Kitchen facilities
- Disease control & vaccination
- Isolation & contagious disease outbreaks
- Records of dogs boarded
- Supervision
- Exercise
- Fire & emergency precautions

Like the application process, the licence conditions can vary between areas. Most councils use the same document, the 'LACORS Model Licence Conditions for Home Boarding (Dogs)', as the basis for the conditions, but they may have made alterations or additions. Updated licence conditions are due to be published in 2017, and it's likely councils will gradually adopt these.

You should be able to find a downloadable copy of the conditions that apply in your area on your local council's website; getting a copy should be one of the first things you do when thinking about starting a boarding business. You'll find the licensing conditions frequently mentioned throughout this guide as they form the basis of how you will need to run your business to comply with the legislation.

Applying for a licence

You apply for a licence through your local council. In many cases you can do this online and their website will include information on the process, cost and conditions and an application form.

Rather than just submitting an application once you are ready to start, it's a good idea to get in touch with the council's licensing department when you first think about starting a business so you can discuss the requirements with them and pick up tips to help you with the process. They'll also be able to tell you how long they usually take to process a licence. Most applications take between 4–6 weeks, but some councils maybe quicker, or slower if they have a backlog.

The cost of a licence varies greatly between councils from around £50–200 per year. Some councils charge home boarders the same rate as kennels, others make allowance for the fact they are operating on a much smaller scale. In some cases the application fee may be higher to cover the cost of a vet attending the initial inspection, and after that annual renewal is a lower rate. In most cases licences are renewed annually and run from January to December; you may or may not get a discount for applying part way through the year.

Inspections

Usually the initial inspection is carried out by a veterinary surgeon and possibly an officer from the council. Renewal inspections may just be a council officer; depending on the council, this may be a dog warden, environmental health officer or member of the licensing team.

The inspector will look at your home including the garden, food storage and preparation area, and sleeping areas, and will ask questions such as how you will dispose of dog waste and how you'll record information about dogs. They are looking to see if your home will provide a safe and suitable environment for dogs that stay with you. Although the idea of someone looking around your home may be a little unpleasant the inspectors are generally friendly and approachable and will be happy to answer questions and offer advice on meeting the licensing requirements.

Criminal record check

Your local council may carry out a criminal record check as part of your boarding licence application to check that you are not banned from keeping animals or have any other convictions that would make you unsuitable to work as a boarder.

In addition to this, some boarders choose to obtain a certificate showing any spent and unspent convictions, cautions, reprimands and final warnings (or the lack of). This used to be known as a Criminal Records Bureau (CRB) check, but is now called Disclosure and Barring Service (DBS) check. You are not legally required to have a certificate but some home boarders like to have them to reassure potential clients of their trustworthiness. They are more important if you also offer dog walking and are going to have keys to access a client's home to collect dogs when they aren't present.

If you want a separate DBS certificate, you can apply for a Basic Disclosure which shows unspent convictions through Disclosure Scotland (you don't have to be from Scotland to use this service), which costs around £25. Or in Northern Ireland, you can apply through AccessNI. Individuals cannot apply directly for standard and enhanced checks, which also provide information on spent convictions, but you can apply through an umbrella body.

Do you really need a licence?

It may be tempting to avoid the time and expense of obtaining a licence, and you may even know of other boarders operating locally without one. However, not getting a licence can have serious consequences. The penalty for operating without a licence is a fine of up to £500 and/or a three-month prison sentence. At best you'll be asked to register, and presuming you pass inspection you may still have to shut down your business for 4–6 weeks while the application is processed. Imagine this happening at the busiest time of year!

What is the licensing process like?

"Applying for a boarding licence can seem daunting; so much of it is aimed more at commercial boarding kennels. But if my home was good enough for my own dog, it should be ok for other people's. The vet inspection is more nerve-racking, but they are mostly concerned with the animal's welfare and safety - a secure exercise area/back garden, appropriate first aid kit, hygienic & secure storage of animal feed, satisfactory arrangements for isolation in case of illness. They were concerned a dog might jump over an area of slightly lower fencing (most of it is 6ft) so I just needed to raise the height."

- Carole Morgan, Chez Jasper

"For me the process was very simple through Wiltshire County Council. I am lucky to have a very nice Dog Warden, who is realistic and says he is there to help people to get a license not stop them, so he'll give guidance on what to do, rather than say no because I haven't ticked all the boxes."

- Lyndsay Moon, Happy Doggy Daycare

"I found the process very easy. Complete all the Council paperwork and then your house and property are inspected, the size of the house and grounds etc determine how many dogs you can board. The inspector gives advice as he inspects. The inspector tells you there and then if he considers the property and yourself are suitable. They also insist on a totally separate area for storing dog food/bowls and preparing their meals. I'm lucky as I have a utility and separate fridge for my fur guests. You then receive your License and their vast "rules" which must be adhered too. All dogs must have their own separate sleeping area (room) and all doors must have dog gates on. "

- Linda Derosa , Dinky Dogz Home Boarding

If you don't get a licence it's a case of when, not if, you'll be caught. Anyone can report you – an annoyed neighbour, a disgruntled customer, a competitor – a proactive animal welfare officer may even check for boarders advertising in their area. Not having a licence can also invalidate your insurance, so not only will you be paying for something you can't make use of, you could also end up with a big bill if something happens to a dog in your care.

If you are now panicking because you have already started boarding and haven't yet obtained a licence the best option is to get in touch with your local council and discuss it. They are more likely to be helpful if you approach them yourself rather than wait to be reported. I haven't heard of anyone who self-reported receiving a fine. Councils will generally try to work with you to minimise disruption to your business while making sure they carry out their duties. They don't want to stop you trading, they just have to make sure you are doing it within the law.

Business Insurance

Insurance protects you from claims arising from running your boarding business, for example if someone sues you for something that happens to their dog while in your care. Obtaining insurance is also usually a condition of your boarding licence. There are a range of types of insurance that cover different eventualities. At a minimum you should have:

- **Public Liability**, which covers you against claims and legal costs from third parties if a dog in your care causes an accident or injury or damages someone else's property. This does not include damage to your own property or loss or injury of the dog in your care.
- **Liability to Animals in your Care, Custody and Control**, which is specifically for people working with animals. It may include cover for: veterinary fees, death of a dog, loss from theft or straying, costs for advertising/rewards for lost dog and dogs during transit. Generally, this insurance doesn't cover vet fees for issues unrelated to boarding; these costs are the responsibility of the dog owner.

Together these two types of insurance cover you for damage to other people and their property and damage to the dog where you are liable. For example, imagine your accidently leave your garden gate open and a dog runs into the road and causes a traffic collision. Your **Public Liability** insurance covers any injuries to the motorists or damage to their vehicles and your **Care, Custody and Control** insurance covers any injury to the dog.

There are a range of other insurance options in addition to this, including;

- **Non-Negligent Harm**, which is cover for accidental injuries or loss of dog in your care that is not your fault, i.e. not a result of your lack of care or due diligence. Although you wouldn't legally be liable for claims in these circumstances, insurance can give you and owners peace of mind that costs are covered in the event of an accident outside your control.
- **Professional Indemnity**, which covers you for claims of damage caused by your professional negligence. This is a useful addition if you offer advice or training alongside boarding as it covers harm resulting from incorrect advice e.g. if you gave an owner tips on diet that made their dog sick.
- **Personal Accident Cover**, which covers you for accidents while working that affect your ability to work and therefore your income. If you would struggle to cope financially if you broke your leg while walking a dog and couldn't take boarding clients this can give you peace of mind. However, it only covers you for accidents while working; if being unable to work is a worry for you then you might like to consider Income Protection insurance to cover more eventualities.
- **Equipment Cover**, which covers equipment you use in the course of your business against loss or damage. Dog boarders don't necessarily have a lot of equipment so it may not apply to you. Consider the policy's excess – if you have to pay the first £100 of a claim then items like dog beds, crates and leads would cost less to replace yourself than making a claim.
- **Property Damage**, which covers damage to your property arising as a result of your business, for example if a dog destroyed your sofa. You should check what your standard home insurance will and won't cover before deciding if you need this.
- **Loss of Licence Cover**, which provides compensation if you lose or are refused a renewal of your licence, but this will only pay out if the reason is beyond your control. In other words, if your licence is revoked because you make a decision that breaches your licence conditions, for example by taking too many dogs, you won't be covered.

If you employ staff you'll also need **Employers Liability Insurance** and if you have keys for a client's house to pick up dogs you'll need **Loss of Key Cover**.

All these insurance options may seem very confusing but several companies offer packages specifically aimed at dog boarders which combine the basic requirements and offer the others as additional options. If you provide any extra services such as separate walking or transporting dogs make sure your insurance covers these too.

Remember that insurance may help with legal costs or claims for compensation, but it will not stop you being liable for prosecution under law.

Choosing a boarding insurance provider

Insurance companies offer a range of different packages to suit boarders. If they don't advertise exactly what you want then call and they will usually adjust a policy to suit your needs. It's important you read the policy documents closely as cover with the same name from different companies may have different conditions attached.

The first step is to call and ask for a quote or fill in online quote forms for at least 2–3 companies offering boarding insurance. Then compare the package they offer and the price. Some keys points to look for include the conditions, exclusions, cover amount and excess.

Conditions

Conditions are terms you must comply with to make your insurance valid. For example:

> *The Insured shall take all reasonable care to observe and comply with statutory or local authority laws, obligations and requirement.* – Petplan

This means if you forget to renew your boarding licence, you may invalidate your insurance policy.

Conditions also set out such things as when you must notify the insurer of a problem and any precautions you need to take to prevent a problem happening, such as fitting smoke alarms. It's important you are careful to comply with all the conditions, as breaching the conditions means the insurance company may refuse your claim.

Exclusions

Exclusions are the things the insurance won't cover. There are usually general exclusions that apply to the whole policy; for example, you are usually not covered for radioactive fallout! Then each section will have specific exclusions that apply to it; for example, this is a common exclusion in regards to vets' fees:

> *We will not pay for the following: The cost of any treatment for an injury that happened or an illness that first showed clinical signs before the start of boarding.* – Pet Business Insurance

WORKSHEET

Choosing an Insurance Provider

Use the chart below to compare insurance providers. Make a note of what their cover includes, how much you are covered for and how much it will cost. Then decide which will best meet your needs.

	Provider 1		Provider 2		Provider 3	
Company Name						
	Cover	Excess	Cover	Excess	Cover	Excess
Public Liability						
Care, Custody & Control						
Veterinary Fees						
Death of Animal						
Loss by Theft or Straying						
Loss of Boarding Fees						
Advertising and Reward						
Animals in Transit						
Maximum Total Benefit						
Non-Negligent Cover						
Professional Indemnity						
Personal Accident Cover						
Equipment Cover						
Property Damage						
Loss of Licence Cover						
Lose/Theft of Keys Cover						
Activities Covered						
Overnight boarding						
Transporting animals						
Dog walking						
Day care						
Maximum Number of Dogs						
Cost of Policy						

Cover amount

Depending on the insurance policy the amount the company pays out may be per animal, per claim, per year or per lifetime of the policy so check carefully that the total amount will cover any likely costs and that you'll be covered if you are unlucky enough to have to claim more than once.

Excess

The insurance policy excess is the amount of each claim that you have to pay. For example, if your policy excess is £100 and an injury to a dog resulted in an £800 vet bill, you would have to pay the first £100 and the insurance company would pay the remaining £700.

You may be able to adjust the excess amount; raising the excess can lower the cost of insurance, though it does mean you have to pay more towards a claim if something does happen.

Payment terms

Policies are generally renewed annually. Many companies will allow you to split the cost of a 12-month premium into monthly payments, although there may be an additional charge for doing so.

Effect of boarding on other insurance policies

If you have existing insurance policies for home insurance and car insurance you should check whether starting a boarding business will affect them.

Building and contents insurance

It's important you inform your home insurance company that you are planning to run a business from home. Standard policies only cover domestic use and in some cases working from home can invalidate them. Your current company should be able to amend your policy to cover you, but there may be an extra charge for this. You may like to shop around and see if you are getting the best deal.

Car insurance

You will need to inform your car insurance provider if you use your car in the course of your business, for example to collect dogs or to transport them to a vet or walking areas. Your insurance policy will need to be adjusted to include 'business use' rather than the standard 'social and commuting'. Your car insurance will still only cover the standard circumstances like injuries to yourself or others and damage to vehicles, not the dogs in your car. To cover dogs you'll need to make sure your home boarding business insurance covers transporting animals. Even if you don't use your car in the course of your business you may still need to inform your car insurance company that you've changed jobs.

Dog Legislation

There are numerous laws that apply to people that are caring for dogs. It's important that you know your rights and responsibilities, to help protect yourself and the dogs in your care, as well as members of the public you meet in the course of your work.

Dog fouling

Relevant legislation:

- Public Spaces Protection Orders (England & Wales)
- The Dog Fouling (Scotland) Act 2003
- Clean Neighbourhoods and Environment Act (Northern Ireland) 2011

Picking up and appropriately disposing of dog mess is compulsory in all areas of the UK, with very few exceptions. In most places councils issue fixed fines to anyone who doesn't comply, and not noticing your dog pooped is not a valid defence. The rules in your area may go beyond just picking up mess; for example, Daventry District Council has a Public Spaces Protection Order which requires:

> *A person in charge of a dog on land to which this order applies must have with him an appropriate means to pick up dog faeces deposited by that dog [...] The obligation is complied with if, after a request from an authorised officer, the person in charge of the dog produces an appropriate means to pick up dog faeces.*

In other words, in this area it's an offence to not have something to pick up faeces with e.g. a poop bag, even if the dog you are walking doesn't actually leave any on that occasion, so you must always carry spare bags.

Access restrictions

Relevant legislation:

- Public Spaces Protection Orders (England & Wales)
- Clean Neighbourhoods and Environment Act (Northern Ireland) 2011

These pieces of legislation allow councils to places limits on dogs in public areas, including:

- Banning dogs completely from certain areas or at certain times
- Requiring dogs be kept on a lead
- Limiting the number of dogs that can be walked at once

For example, Portsmouth City Council has issued a Public Spaces Protection Order which makes it an offence to:

> *... allow a dog under your control to enter those parts of Southsea Beach designated under the Order between 1 March and 30 September inclusive in any year.*

The order includes a map showing the areas that it applies to.

Some of these limits may affect the services you can offer so you need to find out if they are used in the area around where you live. The penalties for breaching them can be quite steep, so check carefully to avoid hefty fines which will cut into your profits. Councils have to let people know about the orders, so there should be signs and the details will be published on their website.

There is currently no equivalent legislation in Scotland, although the Scottish Outdoor Access Code which applies across the whole of Scotland has some specific restrictions for dog walkers including:

> *During the breeding season (usually April–July) keep your dog on a short lead or close at heel in areas such as moorland, forests, grasslands, loch shores and the sea shore to avoid disturbing birds that nest on or near the ground.*

The Road Traffic Act 1988
The Road Traffic Act makes it an offence to "cause or permit a dog to be on a designated road without the dog being held on a lead".

Dog identification
Relevant Legislation:

- The Control of Dogs Order 1992
- Microchipping of Dogs Regulations 2015 (England, Wales & Scotland)
- Dogs (Amendment) Act (Northern Ireland) 2011

It's mandatory across the UK for any dog in a public place to wear a collar with the name and address of the owner on it or on an attached tag. While it's not a legal requirement, many boarders add an additional tag while a dog is in their care with their contact information. As the owners may be on holiday and out of contact this makes it easier for a lost dog to be tracked back to the boarder.

In addition, it's now compulsory for all dogs across the UK to be microchipped. In this case the legislation specifically puts the duty on the 'keeper' of the dog (the person with whom it normally resides) to get it chipped. This means a dog boarder shouldn't face a penalty if they are discovered to be caring for an unchipped dog; however, a chip can make a big difference to the likelihood of a straying dog being returned to the owner, so confirming that dogs are chipped and the owner has checked the contact details are up to date could be part of your pre-boarding checklist.

Nuisance and dangerous dogs

Byelaws on noise
Noise issues are dealt with through local byelaws; if the dogs in your care cause a serious nuisance to your neighbours then your local council can serve a Noise Abatement Notice. Not complying with the notice can result in fines. It can also trigger the council to consider requiring you to apply for planning permission for change of use.

Animals Act 1971
This act makes you liable for damages caused while a dog is in your care. It's one of the reasons that home boarders should always have liability insurance

Dangerous Dogs
Relevant legislation:

- Dangerous Dogs Act (1997) (England, Wales & Scotland)
  - Anti-social Behaviour, Crime and Policing Act 2014 (England & Wales)
  - The Control of Dogs (Scotland) Act 2010
- The Dangerous Dogs (Northern Ireland) Order 1991
  - Dogs (Amendment) Act (Northern Ireland) 2011
  - Control of Dogs Regulations 1998 (Northern Ireland)

Under dangerous dogs legislation, it is a criminal offence for the person in charge of a dog to allow it to be dangerously out of control. If a dog bites a person, this is usually considered to be 'out of control' but it doesn't have to bite for the criteria to be met. The law also applies if the dog's behaviour gave someone reasonable grounds to feel it may cause them injury. The original legislation only applied to being out of control in a public place, but it has been amended across the UK to extend this to private property. This means you could now be held liable if a dog in your care injured or threatened someone visiting your home as well as while out walking.

What you should do to comply with this act:

- Quiz owners carefully on their dog's behaviour and whether they have any history of aggression
- Prevent contact between dogs and people coming to your door, for example with a second barrier between dogs and the door
- Ensure your garden is secure
- Be careful of how dogs greet people when visiting your home or when you are out walking

Breed Restrictions

There are four types of dogs that are banned across the UK:

- Pit Bull Terrier
- Japanese Tosa
- Dogo Argentino
- Fila Braziliero

Owners of these dogs can obtain an exemption certificate which allows them to keep the dog providing they meet certain conditions. One of the conditions of an Animal Boarding Licence is that dogs registered in this way are not accepted for boarding.

Under the Control of Dogs Regulations 1998, which only apply to Northern Ireland, the following breeds are automatically subject to control orders:

- American Pit Bull Terrier
- Bulldog
- Bull Mastiff
- Dobermann Pinscher
- English Bull Terrier
- German Shepherd (Alsatian)
- Japanese Akita
- Japanese Tosa
- Rhodesian Ridgeback
- Rottweiler
- Staffordshire Bull Terrier

This means they can't be in a public place unless they are muzzled and on a sufficiently strong lead (not exceeding one metre in length), held by a person over the age of sixteen years who is capable of controlling the said dog.

Livestock

- Dogs (Protection of Livestock) Act 1953
- The Dogs (Northern Ireland) Order 1983

This legislation makes it an offence for a dog to attack or chase livestock, or be out of control in a field in which there are sheep. This means where possible you should avoid walking dogs through fields containing livestock. If you do walk in or near livestock, dogs should be on a short lead under close control. The offence applies to the person in charge of the dog at the time, not just the owner.

Farmers have the right to protect their livestock from dogs, even to the extent of shooting the dog in some circumstances so this is particularly important to consider when deciding appropriate places for dog walking.

Dog welfare
- Animal Welfare Act 2006 (England & Wales)
- Animal Health and Welfare (Scotland) Act 2006
- Welfare of Animals Act (Northern Ireland) 2011

Animal welfare legislation places a duty of care on people caring for animals not only to step in if an animal is suffering but to prevent harm by ensuring animals needs are met. The needs are defined as:

- a suitable environment,
- a suitable diet,
- to be able to exhibit normal behaviour patterns,
- to be housed with, or apart from, other animals, and
- to be protected from pain, suffering, injury and disease.

Crucially the needs aren't just physical ones but also related to psychological well-being which is why the act includes the provision to ensure animals can exhibit normal behaviour patterns. This means providing space and the facilities for exercise and play.

While a dog is in your care you are considered 'the person responsible for the animal' for the purposes of the act, which means you have the same legal duty of care as the owner. That means, for example, that if a dog is injured you have a duty of care to obtain veterinary attention rather than waiting for the owner to return.

Practical guidance on meeting the five needs are set out in the Code of Practice for the Welfare of Dogs. This is written in plain English rather than legal speak. Much of it is common sense information that experienced dog owners will already do as routine, but it's important to read through and make sure you do have it all covered as these are legal requirements. The information on what is legally considered to be appropriate diet and living accommodation will also inform your business practices.

3

Skills and Training

As a home boarder you will need the skills to care for a wide range of dogs with different needs. You'll often work with dogs that are unsettled, may have less or different training than you'd provide your own pets and may generally require a little extra understanding. The more you develop your skills through training, qualifications, hands-on experience and networking with other dog professionals, the higher quality of service you'll be able to provide.

Qualifications

There is no legal requirement for home boarders to hold formal qualifications but these can be a way of acquiring valuable information that will help you provide better care for the dogs you board and may mean you can charge a premium for your service. Qualifications can also be a way to demonstrate the skills and knowledge you have built up if you want to work in other animal-related fields at a later date.

Courses specifically for home boarders

Several organisations offer courses specifically aimed at pet sitters and dog boarders, which include topics such as business skills, nutrition, basic first aid, health and welfare. These can be a good way to cover some of the basics, although they are based on written information rather than practical skills and will not necessarily be recognised by future employers if you want to change jobs. Courses cost in the region of £200–300.

Providers include:

- NarpsUK
- Animal Jobs Direct
- The Cambridge Institute of Dog Behaviour & Training (CIDBT)

Certificate / Diploma in Animal Care (City & Guilds)

This is a nationally recognised qualification that is applicable for a range of jobs in the animal care sector including grooming, kennel/cattery work, and rescue. It's available as a Level 2 Certificate or Level 3 Diploma. Level 2 is equivalent to grade A–C GCSE and Level 3 is equivalent to A-Level. It covers general animal care including feeding, diets and accommodation, although you can choose units in order to tailor the course to your interests, such as boarding.

The course usually runs over one year and you'll need to be working with animals during it as it includes a requirement for practical work. It's available online through distance learning or at many local colleges. It costs approximately £1000–£1500 and requires an estimated 360 hours of work to complete.

What training have you found helpful?

"I am canine first aid certified and am hoping to start dog psychology in the near future. I do think having first aid something every dog boarder should have. I did mine through the British College of Canine Studies as a home course."

- Hayley Elliott-Edwards, Scruffy Mutts

"I have done some online training - O.A. Dip Dog Walking and Pet Sitting Professional College Guild of Graduates Register with Distinction which I did find useful."

- Claire Harper, Your Pet Pal

"I am qualified in canine first aid and CPR - I think this should be a compulsory part of obtaining a license - after all dogs are family members. I found it really interesting and am due to attend again this year (I attend every two years). I also have the following: Distinction Certificates in Canine Nutrition, Dogs and the law, and Puppy Training and Distinction Diplomas in Foundations of Canine Behaviour Management, Canine Behaviour and Training, and in Solving Behavioural Problems - these courses have given me so much information."

- Lisa Clark, Birtle Home Boarding

Canine first aid

Canine first aid courses are like human first aid courses but specifically for dogs. They will walk you through planning for medical emergencies, including what first aid items you should keep in a kit, what you should do if a dog is injured and how to perform CPR (resuscitation). Typical courses include:

- First aid kit
- Health & safety
- Dog fights
- CPR
- Controlling bleeding
- Dressings and bandaging
- Spinal injuries
- Shock
- Bites
- Illnesses
- Respiratory problems
- Chocking
- Heat stroke
- Seizures
- Poisons
- Burns
- Drowning

Most courses are run as full-day workshops or a series of evening classes. There are some parts available as online only courses but these will not prepare you nearly as well as practising in person. Face-to-face courses involve practical skills such as practising CPR on dog models designed for the purpose, so you can learn how hard to make chest compressions.

First aid qualifications usually have expiry dates and need renewing at set intervals, e.g. every three years. This is because the recommendations may change over time as scientific knowledge is developed.

Hands-on Experience

Qualifications and written courses can be useful but they don't replace hands-on experience with dogs. If your only experience with caring for dogs is your own family pet, then gaining wider experience with a large range of dogs of different breeds and temperaments will help you provide better care for your boarders. The more time you spend around different dogs the more your experience and confidence will grow. You'll learn from interacting with dogs and from talking with their owners and other professionals. Even if you are an experienced dog owner, there is always more to learn.

Training classes

If you have a dog of your own (or a friend's you can borrow) you could attend dog training classes. Even if your dog has already attended puppy classes and has basic training, advanced classes can help you learn useful techniques and practise dog handling. As prospective clients will meet any resident dogs you have, a well-trained dog will also reflect well on your dog care skills. Recognised training classes, which result in a certificate for you and your dog, include:

- Good Citizen Dog Training Scheme
- APDT Good Companion Awards

Training and classes are also available in other specific skills such as obedience, agility, fly ball and field skills. These can be a fun way to learn more about training and dog handling. Make sure you choose a class in which the trainer uses positive reinforcement.

If you don't have a dog, try asking the organisers of local training courses if you can shadow them or volunteer.

ASK A BOARDER

What skills do you think are essential for boarders?

"Experience in dog training, handling, first aid, and pack handling if having multiple dogs. This all needs to be obtained before considering doing dog home boarding in my opinion. "

- Penny Wight, Penelope Petstop

"Above all patience with the dogs and the owners themselves. To understand that your home can be fouled and peed in! That there will be normal wear and tear of your furniture and doors. To realise that you are constantly cleaning and disinfecting and there is no getting out of it. That you have to run your home and family and the dogs like a well oiled machine. Your own family life revolves around feeding and exercise. There will be no such thing as a 'lie in'. In the summer I am up at 4.30am and have the dogs out in the play paddock by 5am. In the winter up at 6am (security lighting on) and have them out by 6.30am no matter the weather. To treat the business as your job and not as a means of making 'quick' money. It takes dedication and a true love of dogs to keep your business going year after year. To have the ability to build your business and client bank and to treat all with respect. "

- Linda Derosa, Dinky Dogz Home Boarding

Volunteering

Doing voluntary work with a rescue centre is an excellent way to gain more experience working with dogs and benefit from any in-house training they offer. Rescue dogs have a wide variety of backgrounds and may have challenging behaviour; learning to work with these dogs is an excellent way to build skills that you can directly apply to your boarding business.

If you don't plan to immediately start boarding, you could also consider fostering dogs in your home – something many rescue centres use to help dogs build up confidence and social skills to make them more adoptable. Rescue centres provide advice and support to their foster volunteers so you can help out rescue dogs at the same time as gaining experience.

Other volunteering opportunities such as transportation or home checks can also give you skills that translate well to dog boarding.

Other ways to extend your skills

There are many other ways to extend your skills and knowledge, including:

- Reading books
- Attending seminars and talks on dog behaviour
- Following experienced trainers' online blogs
- Using online discussion forums to ask questions
- Attending talks organised by vets, behaviourists or rescue centres
- Attending national or regional pet exhibitions and conferences
- Meeting with dog owners at local social groups.

Trade Associations

There aren't any associations specifically aimed at people boarding dogs in their homes but several associations include home boarders under a wider umbrella of pet care services, including:

- The National Association of Registered Pet Sitters and Dog Walkers (NarpsUK)
- The National Association of Registered Petsitters (NARP)
- The Pet Industry Federation

Joining pet associations can have several benefits including access to training; updates on issues that may affect you or your business such as legislation changes; and the opportunity to have your say in shaping the profession. You should carefully weigh up the membership benefits to see if what they offer will add value to your business.

Local business networks may also be beneficial, even if they aren't pet focused. Business networks provide talks on subjects like marketing, accounts and dealing with customers. They also allow you to make contacts within your local community and may encourage referrals or offer discounts to businesses within the group.

WORKSHEET

Skills Check-up

Complete this skills check-up to identify areas where you need to improve your knowledge and plan for how to do that. You might like to re-evaluate your skills in six months time to check your progress.

Existing Skills & Experience

What previous experience do you have that will help you run your business?

What relevant training/qualifications do you already have?

Strengths & Weaknesses

Grade yourself 1-5 for your skills and knowledge in the following key areas:

Tax & self assessment		Dog body language	
Customer services		Breed characteristics	
Managing accounts		Administering medication	
Relevant legislation		Applying first aid	
Sourcing supplies		Recognising signs of illness	
Marketing		Disease prevention & control	
Risk assessment		Understanding of diet & nutrition	
Managing your time		Dog handling	
Paperwork		Dog behaviour	
Health & safety		Positive dog training	
Emergency procedures		Dog welfare requirements	
Cleaning & hygiene		Socialising dogs with each other	

Developing Skills & Knowledge

How will you improve your skills & knowledge?

4

Market Analysis

In this section we'll consider who the clients for your business could be and what they want from a boarding service. This will help you build a business that meets clients' needs and later to put together an effective marketing plan. We'll also look at your competitors, the businesses already offering services to your potential clients, to see what they are offering and what you'll need to do to successfully compete with them for clients.

Who are Your Potential Customers?

Understanding your target market, that is the people who will use your boarding service, will help you make sure your service will match up with demand in your area and later help you to target your marketing at the right people. For example, there is no point starting a premium boarding service with high rates if the people in your target area are on low incomes.

The important thing here is to be specific – not every dog owner in the UK is in your target market. There are many factors that will limit who will use your service, for example the area they live in and their income; not everyone will want a home boarder rather than a kennel; and not everyone goes on holiday, and of those that do go on holiday, some will take their dog with them. You may also exclude some people when you decide your policies on the type of dogs you will accommodate (see page 49). For example, if you only plan on taking small dogs your target market will only include people with small dogs.

Describing a broad target market might seem good because it gives you more potential clients, but they aren't really potential clients if they'll never use your service. Being too broad makes it more difficult to create a service that suits anyone or, when it comes to marketing, to make adverts that appeal to your specific target audience. You want to focus your time and advertising budget at the people most likely to use your service.

If you have trouble thinking about who will use your service, try working backwards and thinking about who won't be in your target market.

Where will they live?

For a business offering a local service, identifying where people in your target market live is a good place to start. Most people look for a boarder within a convenient travelling distance from their home. Grab a map and note where you are and then look at the places around you. If you live in a densely populated area then your target market may live very locally – perhaps within a 15–20 minute drive. If you live in a more rural area you may need to expand the area for your target market and look at specific towns and villages nearby. You will also need to consider how many dog owners who meet your requirements live in an area; although the high-rise apartments next door may be conveniently local, they may not have many dogs living in them if the tenancy or lease agreements ban pets.

What type of people will use your service?

Consider the type of service you plan to offer. Is it overnight, daytime, short stays, long stays, lots of long walks, for small dogs only? What type of dogs, and their owners, do you think would use your service? Potential clients for day care might have one dog on its own, be working long hours, have a reasonably well-paid job, be below retirement age and be looking for someone

What do dog owners want from a boarding service?

"I find owners are really looking for someone who REALLY cares & makes the home boarding service personal. I aim for the personal touch as the emphasis is 'what their dog would have at home'. I find my customers dogs are their 'children'. I think people are definitely looking for a real dog lover rather than someone running a huge dog business. "

- Kim Knowles, Bertie & Shelby's Home from Home Holiday

"The owners I deal with want a home from home environment, freedom to come and go in the garden when they wish and constant individual care. Leisurely walks in woods, fields and beaches. A warm house with a comfy lap and settee and the feeling of safety (I do look after some very nervous dogs)."

- Janie Wellman, The Wellmans Dog Home Boarding

to give their dog a stimulating day with lots of activities. The idea is to get an idea of what a typical client will be like. Not every client will match this exactly but if you are good at assessing your target market then your clients will have some of those characteristics.

Why will people use your service?

Think about the reasons why people might be looking for a boarding service. Holiday care is an obvious one but there are many other reasons people may need temporary care for their dog including:

- Hospital stays
- Holding events in their home
- Going away for business trips
- Having work done on their house

Someone looking for holiday care once a year may have different requirements to someone that's looking for short-notice care for business trips.

Are there enough people in your target market?

This is a good opportunity for a reality check. Having selected your catchment area and the people within it you think will use your service, consider whether there are enough potential clients to provide you with the income you want.

If you've narrowed your potential target market too much, for example "people with border collies, living within 10 minutes' drive and wanting day care" there may not be enough clients to keep you busy. In that case, you'll need to work out how to widen your target market, perhaps by taking more breeds or increasing your catchment area by offering a collect-and-return service.

What do Your Potential Clients Want?

You know your potential customers want boarding, but what exactly are they looking for that will make them choose one boarding service over another?

There has been an increasing demand for home boarders in recent years, which is a reflection of how attitudes towards pets have changed. Dogs are very much seen as members of the family and their owners are nervous about leaving their precious charges in someone else's hands, as well as feeling guilty about leaving them behind when going on holiday. To allay their concerns they look for boarding facilities that provide more than just a temporary space to house their dog, they want to see some of the same facilities they would look for in their own holiday

Target Market Analysis

Think about the type of people that will use your boarding service and fill in this table. You will need to survey real people in your target group to get accurate answers.

Who are your clients?	
Occupation	Income
Age/gender	Location
How many dogs do they have?	What type of dog do they have?
What other characteristics apply?	How many people are in this group?

What do they want? (To find out what people want you'll need to ask them!)	
What is their priority when choosing a boarder?	What needs do they have your service will meet?

Where can you find them?	
What websites/social media (if any) do they use?	How do they find local businesses?
Who/where do they go for dog advice?	What other businesses do they frequent?

accommodation – pleasant surroundings, knowledgeable and attentive staff, fun activities and excellent food. They want their dogs to relax and enjoy their holiday as much as they do their own. A key 'want' that many pet owners describe is a 'home away from home'.

While you were thinking about who your potential clients were, you probably came up with several different groups and it's likely they will prioritise different aspects of a boarding service. The owner of a dog with behavioural issues might consider the most important thing is your experience with training dogs, whereas a nervous new puppy owner might want to know that you'll keep them updated on how their dog is doing. If you know what your potential customers want, you can make sure your business meets those needs so they'll pick you. When you advertise or talk to them, you can make sure you promote those aspects of your service.

The best way to find out what your potential clients want is to ask them. That means finding local dog owners in your target group and talking to them about what they want from a boarding service. That could be formally with questionnaires or just chatting in the park or the vet's waiting room. Online surveys can work well if you are nervous about approaching people – try asking on local social media groups for dog owners willing to answer a few questions.

Questions you might ask could include:

- Describe your ideal boarding service
- Rank these in order of most important: cost, collect-and-return service, daily text/email updates
- Would you prefer your dog to stay with or apart from other dogs?
- How many walks per day would you expect a boarder to provide?
- How would you decide if a boarder is right for your dog?
- What would you expect a week's dog boarding to cost?

You'll need to find out what motivates your specific target market, and how they prioritise different needs. Some common things that influence dog owner's choice of boarding providers include the following:

- Cost
- Convenience
- Reliability
- Experience and skills
- Amount or location of walks
- Company, or absence, of other dogs

Cost

In the boarding market there are usually budget, average and premium options, you'll need to decide where your business is positioned along the scale. A key question you should think about is: how much is your target market willing to pay for boarding and what will they expect to get for that rate? It's important that the prices you plan to charge match up with the prices your target audience are willing to pay. If they don't you'll have to change one or the other.

Convenience

Most dog owners want a boarder within a reasonable travel distance to where they live – but exactly how far is that? Again this might depend on the area and transport links. Are they willing to travel further for a service that offers more than one they can get locally? Other areas where convenience may play a part include ease of making enquiries, placing bookings, making payments and how flexible you are to their needs.

Your Experience, reliability and trustworthiness

Owners are likely to feel their dog's safety and welfare is a high priority when choosing boarding but exactly what markers do they use to judge this? For example, do they use personal recommendations, online reviews, or face-to-face meetings to judge your trustworthiness? Are qualifications, professional memberships, or experience their priority?

ASK A BOARDER

What research did you do before starting?

"I researched prior to starting to work out whether it would be financially viable or not. I also spoke to competitors in the area to work out if there was any room in the market. The people I spoke to did not mind me doing so as I was upfront, and they were helpful with business information."

- Claire Harper, Your Pet Pal

"I researched the average price charged locally, what local boarders were offering and the best places to advertise locally. I spoke to dog owners I met while walking my dog to find out what they would be looking for. A lot of my regulars came to me by word of mouth."

- Alice Paton, Alice's Home Boarding for Dogs

Specific services

Are there specific services they are looking for beyond boarding, such as someone who will collect and return their dog to their home, day care, short-notice bookings, or a specific number of walks? Find out what services they expect to be included in the fee and what they would pay extra for.

Analysing Your Competitors

The aim of analysing your competitors isn't to copy what they are doing; instead you want to find unfilled gaps in the market and ways to stand out from the crowd. Your competitors are people who offer the same service as you, i.e. other home boarders, but also those who your potential clients may perceive as offering the same services as you, such as boarding kennels and pet sitters.

When analysing your competitors you need to look at:

- What services they offer
- What those services cost
- What their selling points are and what they market as the benefits of their services
- What their strengths and weaknesses are, particularly from a customer's point of view
- Whether there are any parts of the market that your competitors don't cover, such as a niche market that you could target
- How they market their business
- How successful they are, i.e. are they fully booked?

You can find out about your competitors by searching for them online, checking their social media pages, looking for news articles or adverts for them, reading their leaflets or marketing materials and asking local people about them.

You can also talk directly to your competitors when conducting your research. However, don't call or email companies pretending to be a prospective client (or get anyone else to do it for you). Call and introduce yourself, explain you are thinking about setting up a business in the area and ask if they have any advice. Ask if they have time to talk – respect their time. You may find that boarders are happy to talk about their work and have good tips to share. You may even make connections that help you build your business and people you can refer clients to that you can't help. Don't expect or ask them to want to give your details to their clients; most

WORKSHEET

Competitor Analysis

Use this table to help you examine your competitors and the services they offer. Aim to fill in 2-3 direct competitors, e.g. other home boarders, and 2-3 indirect competitors, e.g. kennels or pet sitters.

	Competitor 1		Competitor 2	
Business Name				
What area do they cover?				
What services do they offer?		£		£
		£		£
		£		£
		£		£
		£		£
Strengths What are the good points about their service, facilities or business?				
Weaknesses What issues can you see in what they offer or things that are missing from their service?				
Marketing How and where do they promote their business?				

boarders will only refer clients to people whose reputation they know. If they aren't interested in speaking with you, just thank them for their time and don't be upset if they aren't keen on sharing their prices or policies.

Unique Selling Point

Now you've thought about your potential clients and what they want, and the businesses that are already offering services targeting them, it's time to ask yourself why a potential customer should choose you over the other boarding providers. What can you offer that they cannot get elsewhere?

This unique selling point is different for each boarder. For example, you might offer a large garden, the company of other dogs, proximity to the airport the owner is travelling through or a particular number of walks per day. Home boarders in general also have some unique selling points over other forms of dog boarding, such as kennels and pet sitters, including providing home-like care and being the only or one of a limited number of dogs there. You need to know what makes you a good choice so you can tell potential customers about it.

Don't try to offer everything: you can't offer a premium service AND the cheapest prices; or one-to-one care AND group walks; or instant booking AND pre-stay checks. It's just not possible to do everything and trying to please everyone will mean you end up with a service that doesn't meet anyone's needs. That's not to say you won't offer more than one of these things, but decide your defining feature – the one thing that you want to be known for.

Imagine two dog owners chatting in the park, and one asks the other about your business: "Have you heard of Mel's Dog Boarding Service?" What would you like the first thing they say about you to be?

Yes, she's **great with the dogs,** treats them like they're her own, she even sends them a card on their birthday.

Yes, they have **cheapest prices**, much less expensive than the kennel down the road.

Yes, she's lovely, so **friendly and helpful.** I called her about a problem with my dog and she gave me some great advice.

5

Deciding on Your Policies

If you've been thinking about boarding for a while you might already have thoughts about how you will run your business and what dogs you want to care for. As part of setting up your business you'll need to refine these ideas and decide exactly what your policies will be on issues like pricing and the type of dogs you'll board.

How you decide to run your business is a personal decision, so here I've highlighted some of the issues you need to consider and what options you might choose from. Some policies will be influenced by insurance or legal requirements so you should always make sure you know what regulations apply to you and the specific terms of your insurance policy.

While you don't have to write down your policies, it's very good idea to do so, as it allows you to make decisions ahead of time, not on the spot when someone calls to make an enquiry. They'll also help you when you write your terms and conditions, which form part of the legally binding contract between you and a dog's owner. It's likely that you'll find that your policies develop as you gain experience with boarding, and they, along with your terms and conditions, will need to be adjusted accordingly.

What's the difference between policies and terms and conditions? Here we use policies to describe your personal rules for how you will run your business, and terms and conditions as part of the legal contract between you and clients. You might make an exception in your personal policy, for example boarding a different breed than you would usually, but you can't break your terms and conditions without breaching your contract.

What breeds of dog will you board?

Running your own business means you can pick and choose your clients. There are a lot of different dog breeds covering a whole range of exercise requirements, temperaments, sizes and coat care requirements. Which of these you are comfortable boarding is likely to depend on your experience and preferences as well as other factors, such as:

- The size of your home and garden
- The facilities you have for transporting dogs
- Your own size and strength (it's important you can control dogs that pull on a lead)
- If you have a resident dog, any preferences they have
- The members of your family who live with you

Note: Standard licence conditions prohibit the boarding of any breeds listed in the Dangerous Dogs Act or wolf hybrids.

You may decide you can cater for all dogs or you may want to limit your boarding service to dogs with specific characteristics, for example focusing on only small dogs or only dogs that can cope with a daily five-mile hike.

Try to avoid being too specific, as the more you restrict the type of dog you will board the smaller your potential customer base is. If a lack of skills or knowledge is holding you back, make improving those priorities so you can grow your business faster. You may have a favourite breed, but restricting your boarding service to one breed will make it difficult to find enough customers to make your business viable. It's also important not to assume that because you've had positive experiences with a particular breed that another dog of the same breed will act the same way.

If you are keen to limit yourself to a particular breed then you need to consider the practicalities in your marketing plan and long-term business goals. Perhaps you can turn it into a selling point – some owners may look for boarders who have experience or specialist knowledge in their dog's breed. You could also consider specialising more once your business is more established. For example, if you really only want to care for pugs, be willing to take any small dog while building business and gradually swap to pugs only. Some boarders find that over time they naturally end up with a lot of dogs of similar breeds anyway through recommendations from other dog owners.

Never let someone talk you into boarding a dog you are uncomfortable with just because you don't want to 'discriminate'. You should always feel comfortable in your own home.

Will you accept entire (unneutered) dogs?

You must not board entire male dogs with female dogs that are in season or are due to be in season in order to prevent pregnancy. This applies to dogs from the same family, different families or your own dog.

Standard licence conditions state that:

> *Entire males and bitches in season or due to be in season during the boarding must not be boarded together or boarded with resident dogs.* – Model Licence Conditions

It's a sensible precaution to take this further and not board unneutered dogs of the opposite sex together at all. Bookings may be made months or weeks ahead of boarding and owners may not predict seasons with that level of accuracy. If you do accept bookings for two entire dogs of the opposite sex, you'll need a plan for what to do if the female is unexpectedly in season. You won't be able to follow through on the planned boarding, so you will have to let the owner down and may lose the booking fee. If you place yourself in a position where this is a possibility you should make it very clear to the owner when you take the booking that this may happen.

Only 66% of dogs are neutered (PDSA Paw Report, 2016) so, while you may rule out boarding entire dogs of the opposite sex, excluding entire dogs completely may decrease your potential customer base. You'll need to decide to what extent you are comfortable boarding unneutered dogs. Some boarders are happy to accept entire dogs, others exclude them completely, and some have specific conditions under which they'll board unneutered dogs, such as if:

- They are under six months or under a year old
- They are the only dog present
- They've had a successful test stay
- They are only walked on-lead

Dogs that are entire are more likely to exhibit behaviours such as urine marking, inter-dog aggression and mounting, which may be difficult to manage in a home boarding situation. However, this is not true of all entire dogs, nor does neutering guarantee that a dog won't display these behaviours. Whatever you decide to make your policy, it will still be important to assess an individual dog's suitability to stay in your home.

Will you board puppies?

Young puppies require extra care; they are more likely to have accidents, particularly as they are staying in an unfamiliar place, and they are likely to be still working on their obedience training. The experiences young dogs have are very important to their socialisation so it's important that you make staying with you a positive experience. Of course many boarders feel that getting to cuddle puppies is one of the perks of being a boarder and well worth any extra work.

Boarding a puppy may affect the number of dogs you care for. The original Model Licence Conditions stipulated that puppies (dogs under six months) can't be boarded with other dogs.

What criteria do you have for the dogs you board?

"I don't take any rescues, pups under a year, large dogs, gun dogs, Springers or Labradors! Unless I know them personally or their dog is old and just wants TLC. My emphasis is always on a comfortable stay for all dogs - not being overplayed with by puppies or bounced around with by high energy dogs. People like this, so mainly I do have the pampered pooch whom I will cuddle and carry around all day, let sleep on my bed, give that special treat at just the right time before bedtime. "

- Kim Knowles, Bertie & Shelby's Home from Home Holiday

"They must be housetrained and not destructive in the house, must have a reasonable level of manners and be able to left for short periods. "

- Steph Drake, Total Pet Expert

"All males must be neutered - (unaltered males cause problems with other dogs, they can fight with other males, and try to be leader of the pack, plus they scent mark everywhere in the house, had a few and your house ends up reeking! and they are always "sniffing" at females which can upset particularly the older females). "

- Linda Derosa, Dinky Dogz Home Boarding

However, some local councils have since amended this to allow boarding with other dogs where trial socialisation meetings have been successful:

> *Puppies under six months of age must not be boarded with other dogs, including resident dogs, unless a trial socialisation period with those dogs prior to boarding identified no difficulties, the owner is agreeable to the arrangement and the puppy is suitably vaccinated.*
> – Eden District Council Licence Conditions

It's also worth noting that to meet licensing conditions, all dogs using a boarding service need to have had their vaccinations at least four weeks before boarding or in accordance with the manufacturer's instructions for when immunity is achieved. In practical terms this means that puppies under four months are unlikely to meet the vaccination requirements.

Can you provide care for dogs with special needs?

In the course of running your business you are likely to get enquiries about dogs with a whole range of different needs from behaviour problems to heath issues or age-related mobility problems.

Some common special needs are:

- Giving medication, for example tablets
- Giving injections
- Incontinence issues
- Mobility issues
- Separation anxiety
- Aggression towards other dogs

It's important that you are honest with yourself and dog owners about what you can realistically care for. This will generally be down to your own experience but you can expand on your knowledge through training courses or gaining experience outside of your boarding role – for example through volunteering or shadowing a vet, trainer or groomer.

When a dog has special needs, it's important to gain as much information from the owner as possible about what these entail, how to manage them and what to do if you encounter a problem.

If you are giving medication you should insist the owner provides the original packaging and dosage instructions. Remember you should have the dog's veterinarian recorded so if you are at all unsure contact them and check the medication and dosage. You'll also need to know any potential side effects to watch out for.

How many dogs will you care for at once?

To maximise your income you need to care for as many dogs as possible, but it's important not to lose sight of limits imposed by welfare and legal requirements.

Total number of dogs

Standard licence conditions set out the maximum number of dogs you may be permitted to care for at once; this figure varies across different local authorities, so it's important you find out what applies in your area. The standard condition is:

A maximum of three dogs may be boarded at any one time. The number will be determined by the suitability of the premises including the size and available space. – Model Licence Conditions

How many dogs do you board at once?

"I can take three dogs at any one time from different families - this is what I'm licensed for. I personally think this is enough to look after. I have found that when people come to visit and I haven't got loads of dogs running around the house it means the client knows their dog will get pretty much one-one attention and will be treated exactly how they are at home. People have commented saying that they had been to other places and there was too many dogs running round; I think ratio is definitely important for the client and their dog to be happy. "

- Hayley Corbett, Hayleysbowwows

"I am licensed to board three dogs and I board my day care dog (she boards during the day Monday to Friday and comes in when her owner holidays) with one other. I have many regulars so that might mean I have two on top of my day dog. So no more than three. "

- Janie Wellman, The Wellmans Dog Home Boarding

This is the maximum a council may allow a boarder to have; the total you are permitted may be lower. During the licensing process the inspector will factor in the size of your home and any resident dogs and give a total specific to your business. It is a good idea to contact your local authority at the planning stages of setting up your boarding business and describe your home so they can give you an idea of how many dogs they are likely to permit so you aren't caught unawares after your licence is issued.

You will also need to consider the number of dogs it is practical for you to care for. More dogs boarded means more cleaning, more risk of personality clashes and generally more work. It may also depend on the size and personalities of the individual dogs you are boarding as some are more demanding than others or may have additional needs that increase your work load.

You'll need to think about how many dogs you can safely walk at once, how you will transport them if you travel by car to walking areas and whether there are any clauses in your insurance or local byelaws that limit how many dogs you can walk. Again this may partly depend on the individual dogs – it's much easier to safely control three Chihuahuas pulling on leads than three Great Danes.

Dogs from different families

In addition to the total dogs boarded, licence conditions also dictate whether you can board dogs from different families at once. Like puppies, there is a lot of variation between councils on this condition. The original model licence conditions state:

Only dogs from the same household may be boarded at any one time. – Model Licence Conditions

However, since it was published many councils have altered the conditions to allow dogs from different families to be mixed with some stipulations, such as:

Only dogs from the same household may be boarded at any one time unless the licence holder has secured the specific written consent of each household to confirm that they are content for their dogs to be boarded with others. – Reading Borough Council Licence Conditions

There may also be a limit on the number of families you can mix. Again this is something you need to establish early in your business planning.

Mixing dogs together safely requires skill and experience and comes with additional licence conditions which you'll need to meet. A sensible compromise may be to begin your business boarding dogs from one family and consider expanding further once you have more experience.

If you board more than one dog you'll need:

- Space to separate them if necessary, including when you leave the house.
- Written consent from all the dogs' owners.
- To hold a pre-boarding meeting to check the dogs get along.
- To make sure all dogs are vaccinated against Kennel Cough (Bordetella).

Of course, even if you are permitted to board dogs from different families that doesn't mean you have to. Don't assume that maximising the number of dogs is the route to the highest income; some owners will pay a premium for one-to-one care. Some owners want holiday care

How do you safely mix dogs from different families?

"The visitor comes and meets my dog. I only mix families when I know all the dogs and have seen how they react to other dogs. When they first arrive I keep them in different rooms with the door shut, and then open the door with a gate between them. Finally I open the gate and let them get together. Once they have been for a walk together I have not had any problems. "

- Alice Paton, Alice's Home Boarding for Dogs

"At the prelim meeting you should be able to judge whether the dogs will get on together. I had an elderly boxer dog at the beginning and I would never take in another dog if I felt my dog would be uncomfortable, it was his home too. It can be more difficult if they have widely differing exercise needs. I used to walk all the dogs round the block to make sure my old dog had a short walk & change of scene, and then leave him home while other dogs were taken for a good run/ longer walk. Feeding time can be difficult, I usually feed one in the kitchen and another in my rear porch so they can't swap; dogs must keep to their own diet. Dogs who graze all day cause the greatest difficulty, but they will probably eat at set mealtimes if you take their food up after a short time. Be careful about treats and toys - they can cause squabbles so they may have to do without them during their stay. "

- Carole Morgan, Chez Jasper

where their dog will not mingle with other dogs. This might be personal preference or due to behavioural issues such as aggression towards other dogs.

If you are structured to provide care for multiple dogs and an owner wants to book in a dog without sharing you'll need to decide if accepting the booking will have a negative effect on your income. In quiet times when you are unlikely to be fully booked anyway this may not be an issue but at peak season boarding a single dog when you have room for three cuts your income by two-thirds. You could consider charging a higher rate to balance out the lost income from other bookings you'll have to turn away, but it's unlikely an owner will pay triple the price because you'd usually board three dogs.

Changeover day

Irrespective of the number of dogs or whether you board dogs from different families at some point you'll need to deal with changeover days, when one dog is going home and another arriving. Licence conditions don't have a 'get out' clause for this, the maximum dogs you have in your care should never exceed what's set out on your licence. You will need to time collections and drop offs so that bookings do not have any overlap and you have time to do any necessary cleaning between, allowing for owners that may not be punctual. It's also a good idea to have a backup plan in case the owners are unexpectedly delayed, for example by a cancelled flight.

Will you walk dogs on or off-lead?

You should discuss individual dog's exercise needs with their owners prior to booking to ensure that you can meet their requirements and they are happy with your own policies. One of the points you'll need to agree with owners is under what circumstances, if any, you'll exercise a dog off-lead.

Before you make a decision you should check your insurance policy and boarding licence conditions. It's important that you check the policy wording of your insurance to ensure you are covered for walking off-lead and whether there are any conditions you need to meet to comply with the insurance terms. The standard condition for a boarding licence is:

> *Dogs should be exercised in accordance with the owner's wishes. If dogs are taken off the premises, they must be kept on leads unless the owner has provided written authority.* — Model Licence Conditions

This means that if you plan to walk dogs off-lead then you must have the owner's consent in writing. Many boarders also include a clause specifically highlighting the risks and including a waiver absolving the boarder of any liability for injury or the dog running away. Of course having a waiver still means you need to take all reasonable steps to make sure a dog is safe while off-lead.

Even with the owner's consent you must still use your own judgement to decide whether it is safe to let a specific dog off-lead. A sensible precaution would be to assess their recall in a secure space, such as your garden, with some distractions, first to make sure they do reliably come when called.

If a dog cannot be let off-lead you'll need to ensure you still provide mental and physical stimulation to meet the requirements of the Animal Welfare Act. You may consider using an extendable lead or long line (a long but not automatically contracting lead) if the issue is related to poor recall. These options are not practical for dogs with behavioural issues that mean you need to always be in close control to ensure their safety and that of dogs and people around them.

Your ability to meet a dog's needs may partly depend on the facilities you have at home, if you have a large garden this allows dogs the space to run safely. If you have a small garden and usually rely on off-lead walks to meet dogs' exercise requirements then a high-energy dog that can only be exercised on-lead may not be a suitable fit for your boarding service.

Will you require pre-stay visits?

Staying in a home environment is great for dogs' well-being, but for your well-being you need to be careful about selecting dogs that will fit in with your home and family. To help with this most boarders insist on meeting the dog prior to boarding. This will avoid putting yourself in a position where you meet a dog for the first time when their owner drops them off and discover they are unsuitable in some way. Turning a client away, even for a legitimate reason, when they have arrived to drop off their dog and are about to go away doesn't reflect well on your business and will leave you with a very upset client. If there will be other dogs present, meetings are essential to check they will socialise happily.

In addition to just meeting the dog, you may like to encouraging longer visits for the dog to familiarise themselves with you and your home. For example, you could initially meet up for a walk to see if dogs get along, if that goes well arrange a meeting in your home, then follow up with a one-night stay. An overnight stay is particularly helpful for nervous dogs (or nervous owners) as it gives the best indication how a dog will settle in. They are beneficial for longer bookings too; if a dog doesn't settle well, or has issues with house training, it's easier to accommodate this for a weekend stay than coping for a two-week holiday. Dogs may behave very differently in the unfamiliar environment of a boarder's home compared with how they behave in their own home, or when the owner isn't present.

Common issues that trial visits will help identify include:

- Urinating indoors
- Constant barking
- Destructive behaviour
- Aggression

Do you meet dogs before boarding?

"All potential clients and their dogs come to meet me and my dog first before booking a stay. I do NOT take any dog on the last minute I have not met or not checked vaccination cards. I need to make sure no dog shows signs of aggression and can mix well with other dogs."

- Hayley Corbett, Hayleysbowwows

"Absolutely yes. We would not take a dog without assessment first. "

- Beccy Harris, Doggy Paws Indoors

"We take dogs from more than one household so guests have to be sociable and happy to be around other dogs. ALWAYS have a meet and greet before accepting a dog. We make sure the dog will respond to us and doesn't rely totally on its owner for confidence. If unsure suggest an overnight before committing to a long stay and don't be afraid to say no. I'd rather have a reputation for being selective than someone who accepts any dogs."

- Bev Halstead, Ffoslas Farm Pet Hotel

"An overnight trial stay is essential before any other booking is accepted and the owner needs to be available to collect the dog during the trial if needed."

- Steph Drake, Total Pet Expert

- Not getting along with other dogs
- Crying at night

At some point you will come across a dog that you are not comfortable boarding, and explaining this to the client will be easier if you've made the purpose of pre-stay visits clear from the start. Explain before the visit that they are not just a formality but an important opportunity for both you and the client to decide if the service is suitable. When turning a client down always be polite and professional and if possible provide recommendations for alternative care. It's important to schedule trials to give the client enough time to find an alternative if they don't work out.

How will you cope with emergencies?

Emergencies are much easier to deal with if you plan ahead when you've got the luxury of a clear head and as much time as you need to decide what to do. Hopefully you'll never need to use your plans but if you do, you'll be grateful for them.

Sick or injured Dogs

As part of the licence conditions you should be registered with a veterinary practice that can provide 24-hour care. Unless you live next to a 24-hour veterinary practice you should always have a plan for transporting dogs, as you may have to in an emergency.

Unable to provide care

If you are injured or too sick to provide care, or a family member becomes ill and you need to take time off to be with them, what will you do with the dogs in your care or that are booked in for boarding? You plans might include:

- Leaving a key with a trusted friend or neighbour so they can gain access to your home to care for the dogs in the short term if you are unable to get there, for example to provide food, water or arrange for the dogs to be transported elsewhere.
- Having a friend or family member stay in your home and take over care. If you're considering this option, you'll need to check whether your insurance policy will cover it and how will it affect the contract you have with clients.
- Having an agreement with another local boarder to step in and provide care where possible. You'll need a plan for what to do if they are fully booked.
- Getting in touch with the dog's emergency contact (this should be recorded on their dog information form), and arranging for them to collect the dog.

What services will you offer?

This guide is specifically about running a dog home boarding business, a service that provides overnight care for dogs, but some boarders also choose to provide related services, which help top up their income and covers seasonal quiet periods.

There are many things to consider before adding additional services to your boarding business, including checking that your insurance will cover you for the additional services you plan to provide. It's also important that additional services don't interfere with your main boarding provision. You don't have to make decisions about additional services now. You may find you like different aspects of dog care or naturally expand as you find a gap in the market.

Overnight boarding

Standard home boarding services provide full-time care for dogs, with dogs staying in the boarder's home like a family pet. It is most frequently booked to cover when an owner is away on holiday as an alternative to boarding kennels, although it can cover other events such as home improvements or parties that the dog might find distressing to be home for. Home boarding includes all the walks, meals and play-times necessary to meet an individual dog's needs and owner's requirements.

Day boarding / Day care

Day care services are similar to home boarding but the dog only stays in your home during the day and goes home at night. It's usually used to provide care while owners are out at work, but it can also provide cover for one-off bookings for appointments or events that aren't dog friendly. It provides company and stimulation for dogs that would otherwise be left alone for long periods or for dogs that can't be left alone due to separation anxiety. Operating hours between 8am and 6pm are most common, but it may be split into a morning or afternoon session so dogs are only looked after for part of the day. Day care is different from dog walking, as dogs also spend time in your home, although they usually go out for walks too.

Dog walking

Walks are usually included as part of overnight boarding or day care, but walks can also be a standalone service for dogs that don't stay in your home. Dog walking involves picking a dog up from their home, taking them for a walk, and then returning them to their home. Walks generally last anything from 20 minutes to an hour depending on the dog's and owner's requirements. Dogs maybe walked alone or in groups, with one-to-one walks attracting a premium rate. If the owner is out at work you'll need to hold a copy of their keys and you will need extra insurance to do this.

Dog walking can be a useful addition to your services as it provides regular all year round income. However, you'll need to think carefully about how it could fit around the requirements of your boarding clients, who may not mix with dog walking clients and can't be left alone for extended periods. Some boarders provide full packages for a limited number of clients – year round walking or day care services, and overnight boarding for the same dog's holiday. This gives them a small pool of dogs that they know socialise well and the regular income of walking and day boarding which isn't seasonal.

Dog training

For some owners, coming back from holiday to a better trained dog sounds very appealing, though of course it is much more complicated than this as part of 'dog' training is 'owner' training. Skills you develop learning to train dogs would be useful to any boarder so you could learn more about this area of dog care and include it as a selling point rather than a separate service.

ASK A BOARDER

How do additional services work with boarding?

"We've always done walking, boarding and daycare you just have to be aware of time management and don't be greedy! "

- Hayley Elliott-Edwards, Scruffy Mutts

"I offer day care and dog walking. They are great to add income during quieter holiday boarding times. Vet every dog before you take it on and ask the owner plenty of questions to work out whether the dog is suitable for your set up and experience levels. "

- Penny Wight, Penelope Petstop

"Start small and just concentrate on a couple of services initially. Don't be tempted to take on work just for the money (we've all done that in the early days and mostly regretted it)! Make sure that you take work that you genuinely want to do and that will help your business grow. "

- Steph Drake, Total Pet Expert

Pet taxi

Some boarders offer collect-and-return services where they pick the dog up from home before the holiday and return them to their home afterwards. If you do offer this service it's a good idea to consider whether you'll also want to insist on at least one visit during the booking stage where the dog's owner will view your home. You'll need to prepare your car with the appropriate equipment to transport dogs and make sure your insurance includes cover for transport.

WORKSHEET

Boarding Policies

Use this worksheet to help you think about how you will run your business and as the basis of your terms and conditions. You should always think carefully before making exceptions to your policies.

Services

Name	Description

Neutering

I will board:

☐ Neutered dogs ☐ Unneutered dogs ☐ Unneutered dogs under ___ months

If boarding unneutered dogs, I will prevent pregnancies by only boarding:

☐ Same-sex dogs ☐ One dog at a time ☐ Females not in/due in season

If a female dog is unexpectedly in season I will: ...

Puppies

I will board dogs from age _____ months.

Puppies must be:

☐ House trained ☐ Vaccinated ☐ Not boarded with other dogs

Breeds

I will board:

☐ All dogs ☐ Small dogs ☐ Medium dogs ☐ Large dogs

   These specific breeds: ...

I will <u>not</u> board: ...

Boarding Policies (continued)

WORKSHEET

Special Needs

I have the skills and experience to accept dogs with the following special needs:

☐ Medication (Tablets)   ☐ Dog aggression   ☐ Lack of training
☐ Medication (Injections)   ☐ Incontinence   ☐ Mobility impairments
☐ Separation anxiety   ☐ Poor toilet training ☐ Blind / Deaf

Other: …

Exclusions

I won't accept dog's which have a history of:

☐ Food aggression   ☐ Destructive behaviour ☐ Jumping up at people
☐ Being food/toy possessive ☐ Separation anxiety   ☐ Aggression towards dogs
☐ Aggression towards people ☐ Pulling on lead   ☐ Toileting inside
☐ Poor recall   ☐ Frequent barking   ☐ Escape attempts

Other: …

Number of dogs

I expect to be licensed to board ____ dogs.

I plan to board a maximum of ____ dogs at once, from the same / from mixed families.

Off-Lead Exercise

I will walk dogs off-lead:

☐ Never   ☐ With the owners written permission

I will assess dogs suitability for off-lead exercise by: …

Trial Visits

Dogs will require a pre-stay visit under the following circumstances:

☐ Always   ☐ Before their first stay   ☐ Dog by dog basis
☐ For puppies   ☐ If mixing dogs from multiple families

6

Preparing Your Home and Facilities

Although the point of home boarding is that dogs stay in a normal family home, it's likely you may still need to make a few changes to accommodate the fact that you'll be caring for more dogs than an average household.

Preparing Your Home

You need to ensure your home is safe and comfortable for the dogs staying with you. Keep in mind that canine guests may not follow the same rules or habits as your own dogs – don't assume that just because your dog can't open doors that you won't come across a dog that has mastered the skill.

Your home and garden should be reasonably neat and well maintained – because it makes it easier to keep clean, and also because it will help you present a good impression to prospective clients when they visit you. It's important that the environment is comfortable so consider ventilation and temperature control – particularly how you'll provide heat safely in cold weather and keep rooms cool in summer.

Hygiene

Boarding dogs in your home requires careful attention to cleanliness, as homes are designed for human comfort, not necessarily ease of cleaning like a traditional kennel. You'll need to consider whether your current furnishings will be practical to clean regularly between dogs or whether you need to make any changes.

> *All areas where the dogs have access to, including the kitchen etc. must be kept clean and free from accumulations of dirt and dust and must be kept in such a manner as to be conducive to maintenance of disease control and dog comfort.* – Model Licence Conditions

Flooring can be a particular problem area. Coverings such as carpets are harder to clean thoroughly between dogs and some councils' boarding conditions stipulate impervious coverings such as tile, laminate or lino, particularly in the kitchen. Depending on the type of flooring, a vacuum, carpet cleaner or steam cleaner may be appropriate. Make sure any cleaning products you use are pet safe. When choosing cleaning products consider brands designed for kennels or veterinary practices that are proven to work on potentially contagious diseases that dogs are susceptible to.

Choose soft furnishings – cushions, rugs, chair covers and curtains – that are machine washable so they can easily be cleaned between guests or if soiled. Likewise, sleeping areas for dogs need to be easily cleanable. For example, a plastic bed that can be disinfected and bedding that is machine washable will work better than a large fabric bed that won't fit in your washing machine.

What changes did you make to your home?

"We just had to fit a smoke alarm upstairs. We have a dog of our own and our house was already dog friendly. "

- **Alice Paton, Alice's Home Boarding for Dogs**

"We fenced off some of our garden just for my little boy to play in, so that he doesn't have to share that with the dogs and it's safe and dog wee/poo free. "

- **Claire Harper, Your Pet Pal**

"The only alterations I have made to my home is added safety gates to separate rooms while dishing up food, giving my two a little break as some dogs can be quite full on. "

- **Lisa Clark, Birtle Home Boarding**

"I have two baby gates and had to make my fence higher at one side of the house"

- **Katherine White, Happy Pawz home dog boarding**

Hazards

Part of preparing your home is ensuring there are no potential hazards that could cause injuries. When looking for hazards, try to imagine all of the mischief dogs can get up to and what you'll need to do to prevent it. Boarding licence conditions mention some specific areas for attention, but as each home is different you'll need to be proactive about examining your own home with a critical eye.

> *As far as reasonably practicable all areas/rooms within the home to which boarded dogs have access, must have no physical or chemical hazards that may cause injury to the dogs.*

> *All electrical installations and appliances must be maintained in a safe condition. No dog must be left in a room with loose or trailing cables or wires.*

> *All heating appliances must be free of risk of fire as is reasonably practicable. There must be no use of freestanding gas or oil appliances.* – Model Licence Conditions

Some child-proofing equipment may be useful for dog-proofing such as catches that prevent cupboards being nudged open or cable tidies that protect wires. Think about things dogs may chew, knock over or get caught in. If you want to restrict access to certain areas the barriers you use must themselves be dog proof; for example, ensure that doors and cupboards can't be opened by smart dogs. Barriers should be tall enough to prevent jumping and not have gaps a small dog could wiggle through or a dog get their head stuck in.

Potential hazards might include:

- Cleaning chemicals stored in floor-level cupboards
- A cat flap that a dog could get its head stuck through
- Toxic house plants within chewing reach
- A fireplace without a screen preventing dogs touching hot areas
- Small toys or objects dogs could accidently ingest

Preventing escapes

Making sure that dogs can't escape is vital; as they are new to your home they are unlikely to view it as their territory and will be more prone to straying given the opportunity.

> *Precautions must be in place to ensure that dogs do not escape through any exit door when opened.* – Model Licence Conditions

Keeping dogs confined to your home might sound easy, but some dogs see any open door as an opportunity. A sensible precaution is to have a double door system, so there is always one closed door between any dog and an exit. This might mean having a dog gate across the corridor behind your front door so you can shut dogs on the far side of the gate before opening the front door. Don't rely on a front gate as a 'second door', as you can't guarantee someone hasn't left it open without you realising. Make sure that windows are secured too, particularly if you'll have them open in summer to aid ventilation.

Preparing Your Garden

Gardens are great play spaces for dogs but they can also hide a range of potential hazards. You'll need to check carefully, and recheck regularly, to make sure you offer a safe and secure space.

Fencing

There are no specific regulations on the type of fencing but it must be adequate for the type of dogs you are boarding. The standard licensing conditions state:

> *Fencing must be adequate to offer security to prevent escape and be safe, with no dangerous sharp objects or protrusions. Gates must be able to be locked. – Model Licence Conditions*

In practical terms that means you'll need to:

- Ensure that dogs cannot put their noses through fencing (or people put their hands in) as you could be held liable if a dog in your care bites someone.
- Make sure the bases of fences are secure to prevent digging/wriggling underneath, particularly in areas that are masked by planting.
- Recheck the fence line daily in case there has been any damage.
- Consider attempted theft, not just escape; so ensure that gates lock in a way that cannot easily be opened by intruders and there is nothing outside the garden that makes climbing in easier.
- If the fence belongs to your neighbour, you may want to consider an additional barrier inside the fence line to prevent dogs causing damage.
- Be careful not to position items near the fence that dogs can use as launch pads to climb or jump out, e.g. furniture, bins or storage boxes.
- Consider solid fencing that restricts visibility into your garden; this may help increase security as the public cannot see the dogs running around.

Ponds

Many dogs love water but even shallow ponds can pose serious drowning risks, so access to them needs to be restricted.

If there is a pond, it must be covered to avoid drowning. – Model Licence Conditions

Care should be taken that pond covers don't make the pond more dangerous. An unsupported net can actually increase the risk of drowning as a dog falling or jumping on to it can become tangled up and submerged. Instead covers should either be ridged enough to walk over or domed to prevent them dipping into the water. There are a wide variety of covers aimed at keeping children safe from water which would also be suitable for dogs.

Fencing the pond off from the rest of the garden is another option. In this case the fence should be as secure as garden perimeter fencing i.e. high enough to prevent jumping, not possible to dig under, no sharp pieces and the gate should be locked.

It's not just traditional ponds that could pose a risk. Avoid uncovered containers of water such as water butts or buckets that have filled with rain water which could pose a hazard to any dog small enough to jump in. If you use a paddling pool for water play in hot weather, it should only be used under direct supervision and emptied or covered when not in use.

Standing water

Standing water can pose a health risk, particularly in hot sunny weather, as it can develop types of algae that are dangerous for dogs to ingest. Make sure water containers outside are cleaned regularly, and keep an eye out for anything that collects rainwater such as plant saucers. If you have a water feature, using a pump or fountain to circulate and aerate water will help reduce risks. Standing water such as puddles can also create a reservoir for diseases, so ensure that your garden drains effectively.

Toxic plants

Some plants can cause dogs skin irritations or be toxic if ingested. The Dogs Trust provides an extensive list of possible plant hazards. You'll need to use your judgement to decide whether you need to remove or block access to any specific plants in your garden. If you are unsure, ask your vet for advice.

Other garden hazards

Other potential garden hazards you should check for include:

- Greenhouse glass; avoid thin glass panes where exuberant dogs may crash into them.
- Pesticides, including slug pellets, should not be used on areas where dogs have access and must be stored securely to prevent access.
- Make sure there is shade for hot weather and watch out for areas of paving or tarmac that may heat up in full sun and burn paws.
- Put cane toppers on plant supports (a rounded end that goes on the top of upright sticks so prevent injury).
- Make sure the doors of outbuildings are secured to prevent access to any chemicals, paints or tools stored inside.
- Recheck gardens daily for anything that has been thrown or blown over the fence e.g. deflated balloons or spent fireworks.

Disposing of Waste

You'll need to agree with your local council an appropriate method of disposing of dog waste.

All excreta and soiled material must be removed from all areas used by dogs at least daily and more often if necessary. Disposal facilities for animal waste must be agreed with the Licensing Authority. – Model Licence Conditions

Different councils may have different ideas of what's appropriate and it may also depend on how much waste your boarding service is likely to generate.

Options include:

- Disposing of any dog mess picked up while walking in council dog bins (some areas now allow dog waste to be added to general waste bins).
- Putting waste in sealed plastic bags and then in the general household waste collection.
- Using a specialist waste removal service that provides a separate bin.
- Using a special composting 'dog toilet' that breaks down waste.
- Disposing of waste down the main sewer either by flushing it down a toilet or a fitting a separate access – don't flush plastic bags.

You'll also need to consider how you will clean hard-standing after removing solid waste, for example using suitable disinfectant, a steam cleaner or a pressure washer.

Risk Assessment

Risk assessments are a formal way of considering the hazards you may encounter while running your business, assessing the potential risk they pose and deciding what you should do to mitigate them.

There are five steps to risk assessment: identifying possible dangers (the hazards), deciding who might be harmed and how, estimating the chance of an injury happening (the risk), deciding on any measures to prevent or reduce the risk, and reviewing and updating regularly.

As a home boarder you'll need to consider potential hazards when you're at home, in your garden, out walking and transporting dogs. The risks might be to you or your family, to the dogs in your care, to your clients, to visitors to your home or the people you meet while out walking.

The table below demonstrates the thought process involved in assessing risks. Writing out risk assessments for all hazards is not necessary, but it may help to keep a note of improvements that you are intending to make or demonstrate your safety plans to an inspector.

Hazard	Who might be harmed?	Existing Control Measures	Risk Factor	Additional Control Measures
What is the potential danger?	Is the hazard to you, your family, dogs in your care, visitors to your home, clients, or people you meet while walking dogs?	What safety measures have you already got in place to reduce the chance of harm from the hazard?	What is the likelihood of something happening? Rate it as: • High (could occur quite easily) • Medium (could occur sometimes) • Low (unlikely, although possible)	What else can you reasonably do to reduce the likelihood of the hazard happening or mitigate its effect?
Dogs may escape from garden	Dog	Secure fencing and gate	Medium	Add padlock to gate to make sure it can't be opened without my knowledge
Dog injured while walking	Dog	Safe walking areas and vigilance	Low	Take first aid course to learn how to treat injuries to minimise seriousness

When thinking about risk there are several important considerations you should keep in mind. Dogs' abilities can vary depending on their breed and size; what might be safe for one dog might pose a problem for another. Dogs may not behave in a predictable manner, and likewise members of the public you meet walking can't be relied upon to act responsibly. You should continually reassess potential hazards to ensure the risks are minimised as much as possible.

Fire / Emergency Precautions

As part of your boarding licence conditions you are required to consider the risk of fire and other emergencies and have a plan for the safe evacuation of dogs in your care.

> *A fire warning procedure and emergency evacuation plan – including details of where dogs are to be evacuated to in the event of a fire or other emergency – must be drawn up, brought to the attention of those involved in the home boarding arrangements and/or displayed in a prominent place on the premises. The Licensee must have suitable arrangements for the temporary boarding of dogs in the event that the licensed premise is rendered uninhabitable.* – Model Licence Conditions

You will need to install appropriate fire detection equipment, such as smoke alarms. If you are unsure what would be suitable for your home contact your local Fire Safety Officer via your local fire station. Licence conditions stipulate:

> *The home must have at least 2 working smoke detectors located at the top & bottom of the staircase, or other appropriate location.* – Model Licence Conditions

Make sure that you always know the location of the dogs in the property. Dogs should sleep in an area that can:

> *… be easily evacuated in the event of a fire, without putting the occupiers of the property at risk* – Model Licence Conditions

For example, a downstairs room with a door to the outside is suitable. Remember, you'll also need to be able to open the door so make sure you can access the keys.

If you are evacuating dogs then you need to be able to safely contain them outside if you are unable to access equipment stored inside your home. For example, you could store spare leads in an outbuilding or the garden for emergencies.

Once you've safely evacuated from your home, what will you do with the dogs? Is there a friend or neighbour with a secure room or garden where who could house them in the immediate short term? Do you have access to the dogs' owners and emergency contacts details if you are not able to return to your home immediately? You might keep a password protected online backup of your contacts so you can access it from any internet-connected device.

Emergencies may not be fire related and you may not be home at the time. It could be flooding, gas leaks or that you've been expectedly prevented from returning home and the dogs require care. Licence conditions require that:

> *A relative, friend or neighbour within 5 minutes travelling time must have a spare set of keys and access to the premises in case of an emergency. These details must be made available to the Licensing Authority.* – Model Licence Conditions

You could also consider using a key safe; this is a secure box with an access code that is fitted on the outside of your house with a spare key inside. It means you can give the code to anyone that might need to gain access without them having to track down who has a physical key.

It's important that you have thought about and written down your plans, and that everyone living in your home is clear about what those plans are and any specific roles they have.

Purchasing Equipment

One of the benefits of starting a home boarding business is that you don't need a great deal of equipment. Depending on your policies you may require clients to supply the food, bedding, collar and lead for their dog, further reducing the equipment you'll need.

Next we'll look at some of the equipment you might need. Make a note of what you'll need, and, after comparing prices, where you intend to buy it from and how much it will cost. This will help you when it comes to calculating your start-up costs.

Item	Where you plan to buy	Expected cost	Obtained
Dog gate	Local pet shop	£54.99	

Your own clothing

Three walks a day all year around means you'll need suitable clothing for all weathers that's sturdy enough to stand up to a lot of muddy paws. Waterproof trousers and jacket (preferably with plenty of pockets) are essential for winter and you'll need good quality walking shoes. Some boarders like to have clothing with their company branding on, which can be a good way to market yourself to dog owners while you are out walking. You can buy clothing online that is printed with custom logos but you'll be limited to the styles they stock. If you have a favourite comfortable clothing brand find a local embroidery or printing company and they'll be able to add your logo to clothing you have pre-purchased.

Walking supplies

Although dog owners usually supply their dogs' own collar and lead, you should have spares in case they are lost or damaged.

> *Dogs must wear a collar and identity tag during their time in boarding. The tag must display the name, address and telephone number of the boarding premises.* – Model Licence Conditions

Your licensing conditions may require you to add an identification tag to the dog's collar with your business name and telephone number – that way you are more likely to be reunited with a dog quickly if they are lost. Even if it's not a requirement in your area, it's still a good idea to do this. You can have custom tags engraved relatively cheaply online or in many large pet stores.

While walking, you'll generally need a bag or pockets to carry poop bags, business cards, a spare lead, treats and your phone. What you carry may depend when and where you are walking. In summer you may find a collapsible bowl and water bottle (for you and the dogs) useful too. In winter or late evenings a torch and reflective bands for the dogs and you are good safety precautions.

Bedding

You'll need to decide if you will supply bedding or ask clients to bring it with them. Bedding from home can help dogs settle as it smells familiar but it can also be a carrier for parasites. Even if dogs bring their own bedding, it's helpful to have spares in case of accidents or damage.

First aid kit

A well-stocked first aid kit is compulsory for boarding providers. You can learn more about what you need by attending a canine first aid course and your vet may be able to offer advice and supplies.

Some items you might include are:

- Blunt ended scissors
- Tweezers
- Tick remover
- Medical tape
- Vet wrap
- Tefla Pads (Non-stick dressings)
- Antiseptic wipes
- A muzzle
- Latex gloves
- A blanket (a foil blanket folds small)
- Saline pods (these are sterile pods for washing eyes or wounds)

Your first aid kit should be a suitable box/container that is easy to carry and keeps the contents dry. If you travel by car you could stock a second kit there and you may like to take basic supplies while out walking.

Transportation

If you are going to be transporting dogs, either to suitable walking areas or as part of a collection and delivery service, you'll need to think about how you'll do that safely. You'll need a suitable-sized vehicle with enough space to secure dogs in a dog cage or behind a dog guard while travelling. If you are transporting more than one dog then they should have appropriately sized individual cages. When choosing a cage you should look for one that is designed for use in cars and crash tested, not a standard crate.

Dogs should never be left unsupervised in cars, even for short periods, and journey times should be kept to a minimum. If your car doesn't have air conditioning, you might consider getting it retrofitted to make journeys more comfortable on hot days. Make sure you've discussed car travel with the client so you know how well their dog copes with it.

Office Supplies

You don't have to have a separate office but you'll need some office supplies such as a printer and paper for printing forms. If you keep paper files you'll need somewhere to store them securely, or, if you want to manage clients electronically, a suitable computer with appropriate software.

You'll also need to decide whether you want a separate phone number for business calls. This can be helpful when answering the phone as you'll know whether it's someone calling to chat or a potential client calling and should be answered with a perky 'Hello, Mel's Dog Boarding Service'. It also means you can easily separate out personal and business use when working out your expenses for tax.

There are several ways to do this, you can have an additional landline installed, use two separate mobile phones or a mobile phone that has two sim card slots (a duel sim phone). You can also use an app that adds a second phone number or talk with your mobile contract provider to see what business options they have. It means you can carry one phone but keep your personal calls and business calls separate.

7

Financial Planning

The goal of most business owners is to make a profit, and if you want to succeed at that you need to plan your finances carefully from the start. You'll need to know how much it will cost you to start your business, what costs you'll have on an ongoing basis, how much you can expect to earn and what tax you'll need to pay on that income. Planning your finances before you start trading will help you work out if running a home boarding business does have the potential to provide the income you need to cover your living expenses.

Start-up Costs

Calculating your start-up costs will let you know how much money you need to have available to start your business and how much work you need to do before you'll start earning a profit.

At the start of your business you'll have all the costs associated with setting up but little income, so it's the time you need to be most savvy with your money. Make a distinction between what the essentials are and what would be nice to have. If it's not essential, then buying it could be a longer-term goal once you've started to earn a regular income. Compare prices, consider buying second-hand and don't get carried away in the excitement of a new business and overpay. It's possible to set up a dog boarding business without large start-up costs – but you have to be sensible about spending your money. Don't run up debt paying for billboard adverts, fancy dog beds, new computers or cars for transport. Once you have profits, then you can invest them back into your business if you really need those things. Even if you aren't starting on a tight budget, it is still good business sense to make sure your purchases are justified.

Your start-up costs should include everything that you'll need to get going with your business, including your boarding licence, insurance, equipment such as collar tags and the cost of any changes you need to make to your home.

Start-up Costs

Use this worksheet to itemise your start-up costs and determine whether you have enough funding to cover them.

Item Required	Purchase From	Amount
Boarding Licence Application		
Insurance		
Cleaning Supplies		
Marketing		
Website		
Travel Equipment		
Contingency		
Total		
Funding Sources		**Amount**
Cash		
Loan		
Grant		
Total		

Start-up grants

If you don't have enough savings to cover your start-up expenses you'll need to research business start-up loans and grants to help with the costs. Start-up grants are usually designed to help people who meet specific criteria, such as geographical location, type of business or age. To find grants, try searching online or contacting your local bank, library, council or business network.

If you don't qualify for a grant you may be able to apply for a loan to cover any costs involved in setting up your business. If you do decide to take this route, make sure you have a clear understanding of how much you will owe and when and how you will pay it back if your business doesn't go as expected.

What will you charge for your services?

You should give careful thought to setting your prices, don't just pull a number out of thin air. If your price is too high you will struggle to attract clients and may make less than being fully booked at a lower rate. If your prices are too low you'll have a bigger potential client base but you may not make enough money to provide yourself an income and raising your prices later may upset your established clients. Ideally you want to hit the perfect spot in the middle where you'll have just the right number of clients happy to pay your rate to fill your spaces.

What do your competitors charge?

The price for home boarding in the UK is between £15–30 per day, with around £22 per day being the average. Before you make a decision on prices you should complete your competitor analysis (see page 47), in which you'll record your competitors' prices and services. That will give you a more accurate idea of what prices are like in your local area. Knowing what your competitors charge is important but you don't have to copy them or even undercut them to run a successful business. Being the cheapest can be a selling point, but it also means you need to work harder to make the same amount of money.

Where does your service fit in the market?

It's likely that there are a range of different prices and services in your area from budget through to premium. You'll need to decide where on this scale your business fits. If you want to charge a higher rate than average, then you need to offer added value, or perceived value, to customers so that they can understand the justification for the higher fee.

If you charge about average for boarding in your area then offering some extra value can give people a reason to choose you over others. Value doesn't have to be something physical like free treats; it can be more walks, easier booking or regular updates on their dog. If there is more demand in the area than your competitors can currently meet then you may not need to offer added value – the same value plus your availability will be enough.

How much demand is there for boarding?

Demand is a big factor in pricing. If there are a lot of local home boarders with spaces you'll need to work very hard to justify a price above the average for your local area. If there is a shortage and the service is in high demand then you may be able to fill your slots and charge a premium.

Raising prices will lower demand for your service, but this may not be a bad thing if there is a very high demand in your area and you only want people who will pay premium rates. It might also be that you'd prefer to board fewer dogs but get paid more for each one.

What expenses do you need to cover?

It's important that your prices cover your costs or you won't make any profit. It may help you to divide up your estimated running costs per week or day to give you an average. You need to make sure that the cost of things like food (if you include meals) or petrol and car insurance (if you offer a collection-and-return service) are all factored into your prices.

ASK A BOARDER

Do you have any tips for setting prices?

"You always get people wanting to pay less. Usually it's the enquiries that ask the price straight away... it is far more specialised than kennels and the dogs get way more for the money than most kennels can offer. We do have to make a living out of having only a few dogs."

- Penny Wight, Penelope Petstop

"Think about prices check what other in your area charge. Don't under cut them. Remember it is easier to decrease your prices then it is to increase them."

- Katherine White, Happy Pawz home dog boarding

Setting Prices

There is no magic formula to setting prices, but this worksheet will help you consider some of the key factors in pricing, determine if a price is viable and factor in local market forces.

What do you want to earn?

Think about how much you need to earn to make boarding a viable income for you. You could consider what you need to pay household bills or how much you'd earn in a different job.

My current outgoings:

Mortgage/rent	£
Utility bills	£
Groceries	£
Loans	£
Leisure activities	£
Car & travel costs	£
Other outgoings	£
Business expenses	£
Total per year	£

In my current job I earn:

Hourly wage	£
Hours per week	
Weeks per year	
Total per year	£

The hourly wage I would like to achieve is:

Hourly wage	£
Hours per year (average 1650)	
Total per year	£

What do you need to charge per dog per day to achieve this?

This table will help you calculate what you need to charge per dog per day to achieve your income goal. This will depend on the portion of the time you are fully booked. Try calculating it for different booking levels to see how it changes.

A	What you want to earn per year	£	£	£	£
B	Days per year available to work				
C	Portion of time fully booked	25%	50%	75%	90%
D	Days per year booked (B x C)				
E	Total income per day (A / D)	£	£	£	£
F	Number of dogs				
G	Price per dog per day (E / F)	£	£	£	£

↰ Add, multiply or divide the values of the corresponding lettered boxes.

Setting Prices (continued)

Where does your proposed price fit in the market?

As part of your market research you should consider what your competitors charge and how you will be positioned within the market.

The cost of this service in my local area is:

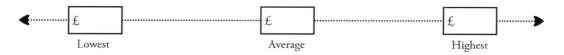

Lowest   Average   Highest

Indicate where on the scale your price will fall. Justify your proposed prices e.g. does your service have additional benefits that justify a price towards the higher end of the market.....

What will your clients be willing to pay?

Before finalising your prices you should talk to people in your potential client base to find out what they are willing or able to pay for a boarding service.

Ask: How much would you expect to pay for this service?

Ask: Do you think this price is good value for money?

How viable is your price?

Use this table to work out what portion of the time you'll need to be fully booked to achieve the income you want at the price per dog per day you have chosen. The higher portion of time you need to be fully booked the less viable your price is - remember no one achieves 100%.

H	Price per dog per day	£
I	Number of dogs	
J	Total income per day (H x I)	£
K	What you want to earn per year	£
L	Days you'll need to work (K / J)	
M	Days per year available to work	
N	**Portion of time you'll need to be fully booked (L / M) x 100**	%

How much is your time worth?

You may like to work out how much you could earn per day in another job, for example working at a boarding kennel, and use that to calculate how much you need to charge to earn an equivalent amount.

Changing prices

You'll need to review your prices over time to keep up with inflation; an annual review in January works well for most boarders. If you plan to do this from the start you can make sure that your repeat clients expect the change as part of normal business practices and aren't put off by a sudden increase. Make sure your records have clear information about what price you quoted for future bookings; for example, if someone booked in December for a holiday in March, know what price they expect to pay. Reviewing your prices means looking at the same factors you used originally to set them, and seeing how your competitors and demand have changed in the past year.

Discounts

Discounts can be a useful incentive for customers but you need to make sure that the benefit you get in extra business is worth more than the reduction in payment. The benefits of discounts can be difficult to quantify but can mean you gain a loyal customer, make someone pick you over another boarder, or make a customer feel like they've got a good deal.

A common discount is to offer a lower price for the second (or more) dog booked in from the same family. This is something you might like to research and see whether other local services offer this; if they don't, it could be your unique selling point (see page 48).

If you do offer a discount, how much you want to offer will probably depend on your business set-up and the demand for your services. If you could easily fill a slot with another dog from a different family at full price then offering a large discount reduces your income. Alternatively if you are limited to only boarding dogs from the same family by your licence conditions then offering a discount to specifically attract multi-dog families can be a good way to boost your income. An attractive-sounding 50% discount still means you are increasing your income by 50% over just boarding a single dog.

Keeping Accounts

It's important that you keep accurate records of your income and expenses – the money you are paid and the cost of anything you buy for your business. You'll need this information when it is time to submit a tax return and pay your tax, and also so that you can see how much money your business is making.

You need to keep records of your business income and outgoings for tax purposes. You'll find it's much easier if you lay out your accounts well from the start and keep on top of them, rather than trying to remember what payments were for months later, when you suddenly realise your tax return is due.

At its most basic, all you need is a written ledger of money going in and coming out of the business. You can buy pre-printed ledger books for recording this from a stationers or office supply store. However, you could also make your own printouts to fill in, which are tailored to how you run your business.

You might prefer to keep accounts on a computer as this makes it easier to edit and update figures, and some of the calculations will be done for you. A spreadsheet program is the most basic option and acts like an electronic version of a ledger. You can use free software such as LibreOffice's Calc or Google Sheets for this. Spreadsheets can be set to do calculations for you, such as adding up a column or calculating percentages.

There are also accounting software packages such as Sage and QuickBooks, which offer more advanced features such as invoicing, receipts and tracking when payments are due, although there may be a fee for their use.

If you find the idea of keeping accounts yourself very daunting, you could hire a bookkeeper to do it for you, but this is the most expensive option.

Accounting period

Your accounts should cover one year at a time, so you start a new ledger or spreadsheet each business year. Your business year will probably not be the same as a calendar year; you can choose any start date, but the tax year runs from 6th April one year to 5th April of the next year, so making your accounts cover the same period makes it easier to fill in your tax return and keep track of what you will owe. The dates of your business year are called your accounting period.

Cash basis vs traditional accounting

Most home boarders use cash basis accounting, which means you only declare money that you have received or paid out, not money which is owed to you or that you owe but haven't yet paid. This makes keeping accounts less complicated than with traditional accounting, which records income and expenses on the date you sent an invoice or were billed for the expense, and has to accommodate payments not received and debts owed.

Having a dedicated bank account

If you are operating as a self-employed sole trader (not a limited company) you don't legally have to have a separate bank account for your business, but there are some good reasons why you might want to:

- It makes it easier to keep your personal and business expenses separate, so when you are doing your accounts you can easily find all of the expenses that you can deduct.
- You can easily see how your business is going, including your income and expenses, and transfer just your 'wage' to your personal account.
- If HM Revenue and Customs (HMRC) ever decides to look at your accounts in more detail, it's much easier to show what is business related.

If you decide you want a second account then there are two options, a standard current account or a business account. Business accounts are similar to personal current accounts but may offer

Do you have any tips for managing accounts?

"I don't really budget for future expenses I just tend to save some each month so I can pay for my license and any other big payouts. Poop bags and biscuits aren't that expensive!"

- Hayley Elliott-Edwards, Scruffy Mutts

"I use pen and paper for my accounts. I have a file which has 12 sections and each month corresponds to each pocket so then when I do my accounts they are all there already separated etc. "

- Lisa Clark, Birtle Home Boarding

"Keep a separate bank account, even if it's personal account. I use online software for accounting (QuickBooks) and for bookings I use an online pet sitting software. The pet sitting software shows me all the money I have coming in and the back account shows me all the money I have going out!"

- Lyndsay Moon, Happy Doggy Daycare

additional options and are necessary for some methods of credit card processing. Some current accounts state in their terms and conditions that they cannot be used for business purposes, and if you are detected as processing a high number of transactions, the bank may close your account or ask you to move to a business one. Another benefit of a business account is that you can use it to trade under your business name – although, unless you are dealing in cheques, no one is likely to see the account name. The downside to a business account is that there is often a charge for the service. Some banks will offer start-ups a limited period of free banking, but make sure you are clear about the charges after this and any charges for processing cheques or other transactions.

Income

Income is any money that comes into the business; for most boarders that will be payments for bookings, but if you have any additional services or sell anything to clients such as treats, all of that needs to be included.

A simple record for income would be something like:

Date Received	Client Name	Payment For	Payment Method	Amount
20/05/2017	Jo Bloggs	50% deposit for booking 01/07/2017–08/07/2017	Bank transfer	£70
21/06/2017	Ann Bloggs	Late collection fee	Cash	£5

You might find it helpful to have a separate record of payments that are owed and when they are due, but they shouldn't be included in your income record until you have received the money.

Expenses

Your expenses are the things your business has spent money on. Many of your expenses will count as 'allowable expenses', which means you can deduct the cost of them from your income before your income tax is calculated, reducing the amount of tax you have to pay.

Examples of expenses that may be allowable include:

- Bank charges for a business account
- Office supplies for business use
- Advertising costs

- Professional fees, e.g., if you hire an accountant
- Software for doing your accounts
- Printer and print supplies for printing contracts
- Dog toys for the dogs you are boarding
- Postage if you send out forms to clients through the post
- Phone calls to clients
- Business card printing
- Boarding licence renewal fee
- Insurance for your business
- Membership of a professional body
- The cost of petrol for travelling to and from the park to walk dogs.

There are strict rules about what you are allowed to claim as an expense; expenses must be for business use. If you use something partly for business and partly for personal use, you can only count a proportion of the cost as a business expense. For example, if you have a mobile phone contract and use it for both personal and business calls, you can only claim the portion of the bill covering business calls.

To make calculating expenses for things that you use partly for personal use and partly for your business easier, HMRC offers a 'simplified expenses' option, which is a set amount that you can claim instead of working out the actual costs for some items. This can be used for the cost of using your vehicle for business and for the cost of utility bills. These rates are subject to change, so check with HMRC for the rate for the current tax year.

To find out more about the expenses you can claim visit the HMRC website.

Estimated expenses
Before you first start boarding, you may find it helpful to make an estimated expenses sheet covering one business year so that you can calculate roughly what your expenses will be. This should include things like insurance and boarding licence fees, which need renewing annually. Your expenses might not be evenly spread throughout the year, so having a good idea of your annual running expenses means you can put money aside for quiet periods or large expenses. Once you've been trading for a year, you can use your previous year's expenses as a guide for what to expect the next year.

Receipts
You will need receipts for all of your expenses and you need to keep these for the same period as your accounts. That means you need to make sure any electronic receipts, such as emails,

will still be accessible in six years' time. You could gather them in a folder on your computer (backed up somewhere else too) or print them out. For paper receipts you may like to have a labelled envelope for each tax year. If the receipt isn't clear, add a note on it stating what it was for so that you can find it easily if you do need to refer to it later. You can also store paper receipts electronically – scan or photograph them and save them in a folder with your electronic receipts. Again, make sure you have a backup.

Tax and National Insurance

Each year you'll need to pay income tax on any profits you make running your business. Self-employed people are taxed via self-assessment; you have to report your income and expenses, and you'll be given a bill for the tax and National Insurance that are due on your profits.

Registering as self-employed

When you start your business you need to register with HMRC as self-employed. Your business is usually considered as 'starting' when you start marketing yourself, such as putting up an advert. Registering is easy; you can register online on the HMRC website and there is no charge. You must register by the October of your business's second tax year or you'll be fined. Don't leave it that long though – register at the start or you may find you have a big tax bill.

As part of registering you'll be given an online account so you can submit your tax return online. A tax return is a form that includes your total income and expenses, as well as a few other facts about you that influence how much tax you pay.

VAT

If your turnover (income before expenses) reaches the mandatory threshold, £83,000 per year at the time of writing, then you must also register for VAT. You can voluntarily register if your turnover is below this threshold, but there is unlikely to be any benefit to this for home boarders who don't buy a lot of goods. You only charge VAT if you are registered.

Tax return

It's your responsibility to give HMRC information about what you earn, and that means filling out a tax return. Once you are registered as self-employed you'll receive a reminder at the end of each tax year. You can fill in a paper tax return, but HMRC increasingly encourages you to fill it in online.

Popular culture likes to make up horror stories about tax season, but unless you have very complicated personal finances you are likely to find filling out your tax return relatively painless.

If you keep good records of your income and expenses, you only have to fill in a few boxes and most of the calculations will be done for you.

You have to submit your return and pay any tax due by 31st January following the end of the tax year on 5th April. However, aim to fill in your return as early as possible so that you can get help with any problems and you have time to ask any questions, find out what tax is due and make the payment without rushing. There is a penalty for submitting your return late.

Profit

Profit is your income minus your expenses. This is the amount that you'll pay tax on. If you fill in a tax return online your profit will be calculated for you, but you'll probably calculate it yourself regularly anyway so that you can see how your business is doing and how much money you have earned.

How much will your tax be?

Tax is due on any income you have above the Personal Allowance. In this case, income means any profit from your business or wages from another job. The Personal Allowance for 2017/18 is £11,500, but it usually changes each year. Your income below this amount is tax free. If you earn over £100,000 the Personal Allowance is reduced.

Income is taxed at the following levels:

Personal Allowance	Up to £11,500	0%
Basic rate	£11,501 to £45,000	20%
Higher rate	£45,001 to £150,000	40%
Additional rate	Over £150,000	45%

The above rates are for 2017/18 and are subject to change.

National Insurance contributions

In addition to tax you will also need to make National Insurance contributions. There are two types – Class 2, which is a set amount per week (currently £2.85), and Class 4, which is calculated as a proportion of your profits over a certain amount (currently 9% on profits between £8,164 and £45,000, and 2% on profits over £45,000). However, the government has announced plans to abolish Class 2 National Insurance in future.

Example Tax Calculation 2017/18

Profit from self-employment	£24,024
minus Personal Allowance	£11,500.00
Total Income on which tax is due:	**£12,524.00**

How we have worked out your income tax

	Amount	Percentage	Total
Pay, pensions, profit, etc.	£12,524.00	x 20%	£2,504.80
plus Class 4 National Insurance contributions	£15,860.00	x 9%	£1,427.40
plus Class 2 National Insurance contributions	(£2.85 per week)		£148.20
Income Tax, Class 2 and Class 4 National Insurance contributions			**£4,080.40**

Estimated payment due by 31 January 2019

You must pay the total of any tax and class 4 NIC due for 2017-18 plus first payment on account due for 2018-19 by 31 January 2019.

2017-18 balancing payment	£4,080.40
1st payment on account for 2018-19 due 31 January 2019	£2,040.20
(Note: 2nd payment of £2,040.20 due 31 July 2019)	
Total due by 31 January 2019	£6,120.60

Paying your tax

Tax and National Insurance payments are due by 31st January following the end of the tax year. However, if your tax bill is over £1,000, HMRC will ask you to make 'payments on account', which shift your payments so you pay your tax bill in advance.

So, instead of finishing your tax year in April 2017 and then paying the tax due in January 2018, you'll pay half of your estimated bill in January 2017, do your tax return in April 2017 and then pay the other half of the estimate in July 2017. If the estimate was lower than your actual tax bill, you'll need to pay the difference by January 2018. The estimate is the amount of tax you paid in the previous year.

So, either in your first year of trading or at the point you start owing over £1,000 in tax, you will have one 150% January tax bill, as you pay the existing year as normal and half of the next. This means it's important to plan ahead, get your tax return done promptly and save enough money to cover it. After that it evens out again and you'll pay your tax bill in two parts, due in July and January.

It's quite complicated to get your head around so here is an example:

Date	Action	Amount Paid
April 2016	Complete 2015/16 tax return – you owe £800	
January 2017	Payment due for April 2015/16 bill	£800
April 2017	Complete 2016/17 tax return – you owe £1,200	
January 2018	Payment due for April 2016/17 bill + 50% of 2017/18's estimated bill	£1,200 + £600
April 2018	Complete 2017/18 tax return – you owe £1,210	
July 2018	Second payment for April 2017/18 estimated bill	£600
January 2019	Balancing payment for April 2017/18 bill + 50% of 2018/19's estimated bill	£10 +£605
April 2019	Complete 2018/19 tax return – you owe £1,250	
July 2019	Second payment for April 2017/18 estimated bill	£605

Retaining accounts

You need to keep your account records for at least six years before disposing of them (accounts for the current tax year and the five preceding years). This is a legal requirement by HMRC. This includes bank statements, receipts and records of payments. This is because HMRC might ask you to show them to prove that the information you submitted in your tax return is correct.

Planning for the Future

As you've seen, it's helpful to have some idea of your costs and expected income so that you can plan ahead and keep on top of your finances.

Tax

Set aside the portion of your monthly income that you'll need to pay in tax. You can leave it in your business account (or an associated savings account) so you don't inadvertently spend it before your tax bill is due. If business is going better than expected, make sure you recalculate how much tax you expect to pay and adjust the amount you put aside appropriately. Very roughly, you should save about 30% of any profit you make over £950 per month towards your tax bill.

Savings accounts

In addition to setting money aside for your future tax bills, it's helpful to have one or more savings accounts that contain money set aside for other purposes, including:

- Predicted expenses, so that you can add regular amounts each month rather than having to cover a large cost like annual insurance out of one month's income.
- Deposits for bookings you haven't yet provided the service for; as you haven't provided the service you may have to return the deposit and keeping it separate will help ensure you don't spend it.
- Savings in case you are unwell and can't provide care; for example, if you break your leg and have to cancel bookings for six weeks you won't have any income. Build up an emergency fund with at least three months of your living expenses to help you cope.

Debt

If your business setup costs will require a loan, make sure that you have a clear idea of how and when you'll be able to pay it back. Think about how many clients you'll need to cover the costs. If you already have personal debts, contact the Citizens Advice Bureau for advice on how to manage them and how starting self-employment may affect repayments.

Retirement

Whether dog boarding is a temporary stop gap or your long-term career, you should give some thought to retirement, even if it's decades away for you. As you are self-employed, you are responsible for your own pension saving so you should get expert advice on types of pensions and how much money to put in one.

WORKSHEET

Financial Planning

Use this worksheet to plan your finances. Estimate the expenses you'll need to save for and your tax liability, and think about how your finances will develop over the short and long term.

Fixed Expenses

Fixed expenses are expenses that stay the same no matter how many dogs your board e.g. your insurance is the same price whether you board one dog or a hundred over the course of a year.

Item		Per Year	Per month
Boarding licence renewal			
Insurance			
A	Total	£	£

Put this amount away in a savings account each month to prepare for annual expenses

Financial Planning (continued)

Variable Expenses

Variable expenses are items you buy for your business that you use in proportion to how many dogs you board. So the more dogs you board the more items you'll buy.

Item	Cost	No. of days supply	Cost per day
Dog Treats			
Poop bags			
Petrol			

B	Total Expenses		£
C	Price you charge per day for boarding		£
D	Profit per day per dog (C - B)		£

Tax Estimate

This table will help your roughly estimate the amount of tax you will need to pay, it doesn't take into account income from other sources or higher rate income tax.

E	Profit from self-employment	£
F	Personal Allowance (£11.500 for 2017/18)	£
G	Total income on which tax is due (E-F)	£
H	Income Tax due at 20% ((G /100) x 20)	£
I	plus Class 4 National Insurance contributions (((E-£8,164)/100) x 9)	£
J	plus Class 2 National Insurance contributions (£2.85 per week)	£148.20
K	Income Tax, Class 2 and Class 4 National Insurance total (H+I+J)	£

Note: If (K) is more than £1000 you will also need to pay another 50% (K / 2) on account.

Financial Planning (continued)

Break even Point

It's helpful to know how many days of boarding you need to do to cover your expenses. This is the point at which your business will start making a profit. Here 'days' refers to the total number of days booked not the number of days you work, so if you have two dogs booked for the same weekend that gives you a total of four days booked.

A	Total Fixed Expenses per year (A)	£
D	Profit per day per dog (D)	£
N	Break even point (A / D)	Days

Profit Forecast

Use this table to forecast your profit over the next three years. You'll need to estimate how many days boarding you'll complete. Hopefully that number will go up as your business becomes established. This assumes one dog per day, if you board more multiply your profit per day by the number of dogs.

Period	Fixed Expenses	Total Days Boarding (O)	Profit Per Day (D)	Total Income (O x D)	Profit
Month 1					
Month 2					
Month 3					
Month 4					
Month 5					
Month 6					
Month 7					
Month 8					
Month 9					
Month 10					
Month 11					
Month 12					
Year 1 Total					
Year 2					
Year 3					

8

Business Documents

When taking a booking you'll need to complete a range of paperwork. To comply with your boarding licence conditions you'll need to keep a 'register' of the dogs that stay with you that includes information about the dog and their owner. You'll also need written permission from your client if you plan to walk dogs off-lead or mix dogs from different families. Finally, you need to agree the terms and conditions of the boarding arrangement including the cost and your cancellation policy.

Dog Information Form

Every client needs to fill in a form that contains detailed information about their dog(s).

The form must record the name, address and contact numbers for:

- The owner
- An emergency contact person to be used if the owner can't be contacted
- The dog's registered veterinary practice

It must also include the following information about each dog:

- Name of dog and microchip number
- A physical description including breed, size, colour, age, gender and whether intact or neutered
- Information about their health, welfare, nutrition and exercise requirements
- Date of last worming treatment
- Dates of current vaccination, medical history and any medical requirements

Example Dog Information Form

Owners Information

Name:

Address:

Phone Number

Mobile Number:

Email Address:

About Your Dog

Name:

Age:

Is your dog neutered?

Breed:

Physical Description:

Emergency Contact

Name:

Address:

Phone Number

Mobile Number:

Email Address:

Microchip No.

Gender:

Size:

Colour:

What's your dog's normal diet and feeding routine?

Does your dog have any food allergies or sensitivities?

What's your dog's preferred sleeping place and bedtime routine?

What's your dog's normal exercise routine?

Is your dog allowed on the furniture?

Your Dog's Behaviour

Are there any things your dog is nervous or fearful of? E.g. fireworks, vacuum cleaners, men in hats, or other dogs?

Does your dog ...

- display possessive behaviour towards toys or food? Yes / No
- jump up at people? Yes / No
- jump fences or otherwise attempt to escape from gardens? Yes / No
- chew, scratch or damage furniture or other fixtures? Yes / No
- become anxious if left alone, even for short periods? Yes / No
- show aggression towards other dogs? Yes / No

- show aggression towards people? Yes / No
- pull on-lead? Yes / No
- toilet in the house? Yes / No

If you have answered yes to any of the above, please give details....

Your Dog's Health

Registered Veterinary Practice   Date of last vaccination:

Name: Date of last worming treatment:

Address: Date of last flea treatment:

Phone Number

Does your dog have any health issues? Yes / No
If yes, please provide details…
Does your dog require any regular medication? Yes / No
If yes, please provide details…

Does your dog have any other medical requirements? Yes / No
If yes, please provide details…

Other Details
Is there anything else I should know about your dog?

Permission
I give permission for:

- The boarder to authorise veterinary treatment for my pet, up to a cost of £....
  You will be responsible for the cost of all vet fees upon your return.
- My dog to be walked off-lead Yes / No
- My dog to be boarded with the resident dog (Scruffy) Yes / No
- Photographs of my dog to be published on the internet Yes / No

Signature
I confirm that the information given in this form is true, complete and accurate.

Owner's signature: Owner's Name: Date:

You'll need to collect any information necessary to help you provide a happy and stress-free stay for the dog; the more you know about the dog's normal routine, likes and dislikes, and rules at home – for example, whether the dog's allowed on sofas or to sleep on beds – the better care you'll be able to provide. It's also helpful to know what commands the owner uses for behaviours like recall. Ask about any health concerns; it may be minor things like a touch of arthritis that doesn't currently require medication but that will be helpful for you to know in

ASK A BOARDER

What are the most important questions to ask about dogs?

"Ask where the dog sleeps... if they say on my bed it means we could be in for a few sleepless nights. Always ask about health, especially allergies after having a guest with a severe reaction, the owner hadn't told us about. We also ask a bit about its background, if rescue etc. Any dislikes, particular routines or specific commands. "

- Bev Halstead, Ffoslas Farm Pet Hotel

"I have a very thorough booking form and questionnaire. I think asking about destruction and fears/phobias are something that should be on all forms, microchip number any medical conditions and any allergies, and how they are around other animals, children etc. "

- Lisa Clark, Birtle Home Boarding

"My Care Agreement, which I fill in on my first meet and greet with the customer and their dogs, comprises all of the necessary information I need for the care of their dogs including: vets, all medical history (I have a separate form for this if on medication), next of kin, food, routines, and treatments re fleas/workers, vaccination status. I have an attached questionnaire which asks questions, i.e. where does your dog sleep and what type of bed, are they sociable with other dogs, people, any fears, phobias and anxieties? With this information, and the hour or so I spend with the owners and their dogs, I form a good idea on their dogs suitability for boarding in my home. "

- Janie Wellman, The Wellmans Dog Home Boarding

case it crops up or gets worse. Stress that little details can make their dog's stay more relaxed; if their dog panics at the sight of poodles but loves interacting with other dogs, you need to know!

Go through the form with the client to make sure they've included all the information you need (and you can read their writing). You might like to make the form available on your website or email it to them to fill in ahead of the booking. Then discuss it and ask any questions when you meet face to face.

Updating information

Some dogs become frequent customers and you may find that filling in a long form that is a duplicate of the information already provided is unnecessary for every stay. For this reason it can be more practical to separate the paperwork for your dog information form from your boarding terms and the dates and cost of a stay.

It's important that the information on the dog information form is kept up to date, as a dog's medical information, behaviour and vaccinations records will change over time. A good compromise may be to revise the dog information form annually. Renewing the information periodically also gives you the opportunity to discuss price increases. If there are any changes in details the record will need to be updated sooner and asking the owner to read through and confirm at each booking would be a sensible precaution. While the dog's details might not have changed, it may be that their emergency contact is on holiday and they need to add a substitute.

You are required to keep records (even those that have been replaced by new ones) for a minimum of two years. If you have paper files, a good option would be to have a 'current' and 'archive' folder and periodically check for any records that are over a year old and move them to the archive.

Consent Forms

Either separately or on your dog information form you'll need to include the necessary permissions to:

- Seek veterinary treatment
- Walk the dog off-lead (if applicable)
- Board with other dogs including resident dogs (if applicable)
- Board with a resident cat (if applicable)
- Take and use photos e.g. share them on social media (if you'd like to)

Veterinary consent

To administer non-emergency treatment, veterinarians need the dog owner's consent or proof that you are authorised to act for them and give consent.

A vet can administer emergency treatment without your or the owner's consent if delaying it would affect the dog's welfare, for example if a dog arrived with a broken leg they may stabilise the patient and administer painkillers, but would wait to get consent to operate if surgery was needed and the time to get consent wouldn't affect the dog's welfare. So if a dog needs emergency care and you're not at home with your records, don't feel you must detour to get them.

> *The client may be the owner of the animal, someone acting with the authority of the owner, or someone with statutory or other appropriate authority. Care should be taken when the owner is not the client. Practice staff should ensure they are satisfied that the person giving consent has the authority to provide consent. The provision of veterinary services creates a contractual relationship under which the veterinary surgeon and/or veterinary nurse should: [...] obtain the client's consent to treatment unless delay would adversely affect the animal's welfare (to give informed consent, clients must be aware of risks).*
> – RCVS Code of Professional Conduct for Veterinary Surgeons

You may also like to clarify what decisions the owner is happy for you to make on their behalf, and when you should contact them or their emergency contact to obtain consent. Some clients may prefer to be contacted about any medical issues straight away, others may be happy for you to use your judgement for minor issues and not interrupt their holiday.

The permission form is also a good opportunity to remind clients that they are liable for any vet fees. As you'll be making decisions, it can also be helpful to know how much the client will authorise you to spend. You don't want to put yourself in the position of authorising treatment for thousands of pounds and the owners returning home with no way to pay.

Your dog information form should specify the dog's regular vet, but make the owners aware you may use a different vet in an emergency. In other words, make sure the form isn't worded such that you only have authorisation for one vet.

Boarding Agreement

Having a written contract or agreement protects both you and the client, and ensures you are both clear about the terms of the arrangement. A boarding contract forms a legal agreement between you and the client, setting out the service that you are obligated to provide and the obligations of the client, such as paying on time or providing details about their dog. The contract applies to both you and the client, so anything you promise to do in the contract, you must carry through on.

The Consumer Contracts (Information, Cancellation and Additional Charges) Regulations 2013 set out the information you must give clients when forming a contract, including:

- The main characteristics of the service
- Your name/business name, address and telephone number
- The total price of the services
- The arrangements for payment
- The dates the contract covers
- Your complaint handling policy
- Information and conditions relating to cancellation
- The existence and conditions of any deposit required

In addition you may want to cover the following:

- What happens if they collect their dog late
- Obligation to provide information and inform you of any changes
- If you use pre-stay visits, what happens if they don't go well
- Anything that will invalidate the contract, such as trying to board a dog that's a banned breed or not providing a vaccination certificate.

Deposit

Most boarders take a deposit (a portion of the boarding fee) on booking to the secure the place. This is to help prevent situations where you turn away other prospective clients because you think you have a booking and the client changes their mind later or doesn't provide the necessary paperwork and you end up with no booking at all. If that happens, you retain the deposit which helps mitigate the impact of the loss of income. When taking a deposit, it's important to do the following:

- Make it clear in the contract when the deposit is due; state, for example, that the booking is not secured until the deposit is paid.
- Specify the amount of the deposit; it's usually either a set fee or a percentage of the total. The most common deposit is 50% of the expected cost of boarding.
- Set out the situations in which the deposit will be returned and the situations where it won't be returned.

- If you can't care for the dog for any reason – e.g. the pre-stay visit doesn't go well – you must return the deposit.
- Remember, the deposit isn't yours until you provide the service so don't spend it, set it aside as you may have to return it.

ASK A BOARDER

What terms & conditions are important to include?

"Important ones for me are that the dogs is good around children and with other dogs, has never been aggressive, is neutered (if male) and can be reliably walked off lead."

- Lyndsay Moon, Happy Doggy Daycare

"Permission to get medical treatment if needed and unable to contact the owner."

- Bev Halstead, Ffoslas Farm Pet Hotel

"My most important terms of boarding are no unneutered males over 9 months (some boarding places are happy to accept anything though. Personal choice for what you feel you can cope with everyday). I also usually only take dogs over 6 months. No bitches in season. No aggressive behaviour to other dogs or humans. I also get signed permission to let any dog off lead and then only do so if proves trustworthy. I always take a deposit to secure bookings. I like to set times of business hours as I have had enquiries up to 10pm at night or 6am and I like to have a day off on Sundays every week from enquiries/ drop offs/ collections."

- Penny Wight, Penelope Petstop

"Some people see the job as a hobby and don't release that you may need the money to pay bills. I now ask for a 40% non refundable deposit to secure any booking as I had people cancel days before the dog was due to arrive."

- Katherine White, Happy Pawz home dog boarding

Payment

The payment terms should set out how much payment is and when it needs to be provided. Make sure your payment terms do the following:

- Make the boarding rate clear, either as a daily rate or the rate for the whole stay, and also note any extra charges that may apply.
- Set out when payment is due. It's usually best to take payments on or just before holiday care starts. Taking payments after you've provided the service increases the risk that clients will not pay or will pay late.
- List the payment methods you accept and any condition attached. For example, you may want to request that payment by cheque be made 7 days before the arrival date to allow time for the cheque to clear.

Cancellation

You should explain the process for cancelling the booking and what this will mean for payment already made, i.e. whether it will be refunded. It's a good idea to cover both the client deciding to cancel and if you decide to cancel. The goal with your cancellation policy is to be fair, but also avoid last-minute cancellations that leave you out of pocket with empty slots at busy times you could have filled. Keep in mind you can be more generous than the contract sets out if you feel the situation warrants it.

The Consumer Cancellation Regulations Act 2013 means that if you form a contract over the phone or online you need to give a 14-day cooling off period for cancellations. If they cancel within 14 days of booking you must return the deposit (unless you've already provided the service). This doesn't apply if you've made the contract face to face. You'll still need to set the terms for cancellation after 14 days.

Specify how much notice you will require for cancellation and what fees will be due. With sufficient notice usually only the deposit is forfeit (you'll need to decide what sufficient notice is). If you book very far in advance then you may want to consider a small deposit or returning part of the deposit for early cancellations where you will be able to refill the space. Generally, short-notice cancellations mean the full amount will be due (this is because you won't have time to fill the slot with another client).

Example Booking Agreement

Your Name
Your Address
Your Dog(s) Names:

Arrival Date
Approximate arrival time
Collection Date
Approximate collection time

Daily boarding rate
Total cost
Deposit amount
Balance amount
Balance due date

Terms and Conditions

These Terms and Conditions set out the agreement between 'you', the owner, and Mel's Boarding Service, 'the boarder'.

Bookings

1. Bookings are not confirmed until the dog information form and the booking agreement are returned along with a deposit of 50% of the total cost of the stay.
2. Bookings are subject to a trial familiarisation session to ensure both parties are satisfied with the arrangement. You or the boarder may cancel the booking by notifying the other party within 48 hours of the session. If bookings are cancelled in this period, the deposit will be refunded.
3. Any outstanding balance is due 7 days before the start of your dog's stay.
4. Boarding fees will not be refunded if you collect your dog early.

Cancellation

5. Your deposit is non-refundable if you cancel your booking.
6. If you cancel within two weeks of the boarding start date, the full amount will be due.

About Your Dog

7. You agree to provide full and accurate information about your dog's needs and notify the boarder of any changes to the details you provide. You must disclose any behaviour that may impact on your dog's care including, but not limited to, aggression, incontinence, destructive behaviour and separation anxiety.

8. All dogs must be up to date with vaccinations, flea treatment and worming, and provide a vaccination certificate at the start of the boarding period.

9. Dogs should arrive clean and healthy, excluding any medical conditions previously notified.

10. The boarder cannot accept dogs that have shown aggression towards people or other animals, or any dogs registered under the Dangerous Dogs Act 1991.

11. The boarder cannot accept any bitches in season or due to be in season during the boarding period.

Your Dog's Stay

12. Sufficient food and supplies must be provided for your dog's stay. Should additional supplies be needed, you agree to reimburse the boarder when you collect your dog.

13. If your dog becomes unwell or has an accident during boarding the boarder will obtain prompt veterinary treatment. You will be liable for the cost of any veterinary treatment.

14. If your dog shows aggression towards the boarder, their family or other dogs, or their behaviour is uncontrollable or an unreasonable nuisance the boarder will contact the emergency contact you specify and ask them to collect your dog. If this is not possible, they will be placed in boarding kennels for the remainder of their stay; you will be liable for the cost of kennels.

I confirm that I am the owner of the above dog(s) and I have read, understood and accept these terms and conditions. I also confirm the information I have supplied is accurate and that I shall make the boarder aware of any changes.

Signature

Name

Attendance Register

As part of the boarding licence conditions you must keep a record of all dogs that are boarded and when. This should reflect actual arrival and departure dates, not bookings (which might be cancelled), so don't fill it in before the stay. A simple log in the format:

Dog's Name	Owner's Name	Arrival Date	Arrival Time	Anticipated Departure Date	Departure Date	Departure Time
Scruffy	Jo Bloggs	10/07/2016	9.45am	24/07/2016	24/07/2016	2.30pm
Bob	Jane Bloggs	21/07/2017	1.30pm	28/01/2017		

Although the licence conditions only require a date for arrival and departure, by including the time this can double up as a record to help you create bills as it will show any late collections that may need charging for.

Medication Records

If you are asked to administer any medication or treatment, you should keep a separate record of what and when you administered. An example record may look like:

Dog's Name	Owner's Name	Date	Time	Treatment Administered
Scruffy	Jo Bloggs	11/07/2016	8am	Eye drops to both eyes

Make sure your dog information form records the medication name and dosage, and that you have the original packaging and instructions for contraindications and any signs to look out for.

Diary

While there is no requirement to keep any other records of a dog's stay, some boarders like to keep a general diary with notes about the dog, for example when you went for walks, if a dog refused a meal, any problems you spotted, or times of vet appointments. Some owners will also appreciate a few notes about what their dog got up to or even a photo, while they are on holiday.

Your Own Pets' Records

If you have pets of your own, you will also need to keep records of their vaccinations, de-worming and parasite treatments. Your vet should be able to advise a suitable schedule. Although your vet will provide vaccination records, if you use over-the-counter treatments for worming and parasites you will need to record the type and date these are given. You will need to be able to provide the information when you are inspected so make sure it's written down in a way that's easy to show to the inspector (not a Post-it note on the fridge).

Example:

Pet's Name	Type of Treatment	Date of Treatment	Next Due

It may be helpful to note the dates for future treatment in your booking calendar or use electronic reminders, so make sure you keep treatments and the record up to date.

Managing Your Availability Calendar

You'll need some sort of chart or calendar to keep track of bookings. It will need to show provisional bookings (dates you've had an enquiry for but not completed the full booking process) and dates that have a confirmed booking. If you take multiple dogs from different families you'll need to be able to tell not just if you have a booking for that date but how many dogs and whether they can be combined with another booking.

It's helpful to have a calendar, either paper or electronic, that shows you all bookings at a glance. If you only take bookings in one place, e.g. an office, then a large wall chart can make it instantly easy to see when you are booked up. If you don't have a set work space or a spare wall, an electronic calendar or diary may work better. Make sure you have a backup in case it's lost.

Remember to block out any dates you don't want to take bookings at the start of the year, such as setting aside a holiday for yourself. It's also a good idea to record dates for other actions you need to take, such as requesting payments. Well-organised dog owners may book holiday boarding months in advance of their actual holiday so there can be a long period between booking and boarding. In that situation you may like to make contact closer to the booking to confirm the dates and make sure there haven't been any changes.

How do you manage bookings?

"I keep track of bookings via calendar/diary, making notes of deposits taken. A booking is only confirmed with 25% deposit which is taken off their bill on collection."

- Kim Knowles, Bertie & Shelby's Home from Home Holiday

"I run a diary manually and have a customer deposit log book. And also have manual accounts books."

- Janie Wellman, The Wellmans Dog Home Boarding

"I use a normal diary for bookings. I use Invoice2go [App for sending invoices] for my confirmations so after I have received a holiday booking form I arrange a meet for us and the customers so their dogs can meet mine we go for a walk, come to the house etc as dogs behave differently inside to out. Then I send them a confirmation with dates booked, deposit amount, and balance etc."

- Hayley Elliott-Edwards, Scruffy Mutts

"I have a diary also I use the calendar on my phone for when I'm out and it links to my iPad."

- Katherine White, Happy Pawz home dog boarding

Managing Your Paperwork

Make sure you keep on top of your paperwork and file it as you produce it. You might find it helpful to have one file per client with all the information about their dog, agreements and past stays. That way when they want to make a booking you can find their previous details easily. You should have the paperwork for any dogs currently staying with you to hand so you can refer to their information form as needed.

You'll find you have some documents that are useful to share with prospective clients such as your boarding licence, insurance documents, criminal record check (if you have one), membership certificates for trade associations, even references from happy customers. To make it easy to show these documents and protect them, consider putting them together in a binder with plastic wallets. Check with your local authority if that meets their requirements for displaying your licence.

Electronic vs paper

It's up to you whether you keep your documents as electronic or paper files. Electronic files are good because they take up less room, can be easily sent to clients via email and are easy to amend. On the other hand, paper files may be easier for your clients to fill in and you don't have to worry about computer problems. Even if you keep some records electronically, it's likely you'll have some paper files too.

> *Where records are computerised, a back-up copy must be kept. The register must also be available to key members of staff of the establishment at all times.* – Model Licence Conditions

Backups are important for electronic files; a good question to ask yourself is: If your computer imploded right now, would you lose data you need? If the answer is yes, you need to improve your backup system. Backups are copies of your important files stored in a separate place, such as an online storage service, a portable hard drive, USB stick, CD or even as printed copies. You also need to think about how often you make a backup – some systems allow for constant updates that create a real-time duplicate while others take a backup at regular intervals such as once a week.

Do I need so much paperwork?

Sometimes you'll look at a pile of paperwork and wonder why you need so much. After all, you can remember a dog's name and surely you don't need that many signatures. However, when you do run into a problem, and, no matter how good a boarder you are, at some point you will run into a problem, you'll be very pleased you have the information in writing, and the owner's signature on your terms and conditions. Not only do written records keep things clear and professional, they can also protect you against legal action or be used if you need to take a client to court over payment.

Data Protection and Confidentiality

Being trusted to keep information private is an important part of your reputation. Any information clients give you, no matter how unimportant it seems, should be treated as confidential. This includes things they tell you unrelated to their boarding booking. It's easy to slip up if you aren't careful. For example if someone strikes up conversion about a dog you are walking, you might find yourself saying "He's lovely isn't he, I'm just looking after him while his owner's in hospital having surgery on her knee." You've just given information away about a client's health they may not want to share. Keep in mind that dogs can be well known by people in their local area, so even though you might think you aren't giving out information that identifies someone, their dog may be enough to let people know who you are talking about.

You also need to be careful about what you say generally about clients to other people. Sharing funny or weird stories might be natural when chatting about dogs but if an owner or someone else can identify someone from them, they may be less amused. If an owner hears that you've been telling people about the person who always insists on calling to say goodnight to their dog, even if you don't say who it is, they may recognise themselves and be embarrassed or upset and you may lose them as a client – and anyone they might tell about your lack of discretion.

The Data Protection Act 1998 governs the use of personal information; personal information means information about living identifiable individuals such as names and addresses. The act includes Data Protection Principles, which set out how you should protect personal information, including that you should:

- **Only obtain it for a specified purpose and not use it for anything other than that reason.** This means that if you collect information to help you provide a boarding service, you can't do anything else with that information, such as use it to send your clients information on an unrelated event you are running.
- **Only collect the information you absolutely need for the purpose you specified.**
- **Make sure the data is accurate and kept up to date.** To do this you might review the information of regular clients annually.
- **Only keep it for as long as you need it for that purpose.** You are required to keep the register information for two years and accounts for seven years. After this you should dispose of the information in a responsible way.
- **Use it in accordance with the rights of the data's subject.** The act also sets out rights including the client's right to view information you hold about them.
- **Make sure no one who isn't authorised can access it.** For written documents this could be using a file cabinet with a lock and for electronic files making sure your computer is password protected and using anti-virus software to protect yourself against intrusions. Make sure you think about confidentiality if your computer is accessed by anyone else, for example if you take it for repairs or it's

used by other family members. If you replace your computer you should make sure that your old one is disposed of in a way that makes retrieving files impossible.

If you share information that causes damage to an individual then ultimately they could sue you for compensation, so it's important to keep the information you are given safe and use it responsibly.

9

Marketing Your Business

Marketing is everything you do to put your business in front of the target market you identified in your market analysis and persuade them that you are the service they should use. Marketing done badly can be an expensive waste of time, so spend some time on planning your campaign – don't just throw an advert together and cross your fingers.

The amount of energy you need to put into marketing will depend on the competition in your area and even the existing contacts you already have. If there is a shortage of boarding services then chatting with dog owners in your local park may supply all the customers you need. If there is competition from other boarders, pet sitting and local kennels, you will need to put more effort into both marketing and persuading the people who see your efforts that you are the person they should choose to care for their dog.

It may take some time to find clients, so it is important to plan ahead. Consult with your local council and check at what point in the licensing process you can start advertising. Have a plan (and some savings) to support you through the initial period when you are starting up. People often book boarders weeks or months ahead of when they need them so you are unlikely to take many bookings for immediate starts.

Logo and Branding

Before you start marketing your business, it's a good idea to decide how you will present yourself to your potential clients. This is called your brand and includes all the things that go into creating the impression client's form of you including your name and logo but also how you interact with clients and the key messages you share.

Making a conscious choice about how you will brand yourself will help you be consistent across all your advertising channels so you are recognisable and stand out from your competition. A consistent message across your marketing also reinforces the message you are trying to convey so it sticks in people's memories. Not everyone in your target market will need boarding at the same time, so you want a dog owner who sees your brand now to remember you if they need boarding at a later date.

The key elements you need to decide on are your name, how you will represent yourself visually (your logo, colours and images), and what message you want potential clients to take away.

Part of your brand may be the visual elements, like colours and a logo, that represent you. Not all home boarders have a graphical logo. Logos can be as simple as your business name written in the same colour and font each time it's used. If you do use a graphic, keep it simple. Simple logos are easier to reproduce, particularly if you want to use them on clothing and business literature where they'll be different sizes and seen at different distances. It's also important that your logo is unique and belongs to you. Don't use clip art or pictures you find online as a logo.

A colour scheme can be an easy way to keep your marketing consistent. Choose one to three colours you like and that convey the impression you want about your business. For example, if your selling point is walks in the countryside you might choose natural-looking greens and browns to represent your business.

As a small business an important part of your brand will be your reputation. Building your reputation is something you will have to do gradually but you can help nurture it by always conducting your business in a professional and friendly manner. As a boarder, when you are promoting your business you are actually promoting yourself. You are your business's best asset, so how you present yourself in public is important. For example, if people see you in the park with happy well-behaved dogs and offering a friendly "good morning" this will help you build a good reputation and may help you get recommendations.

Naming Your Business

Your business name is your identity; it is often the first thing people hear relating to your service so it should make a good first impression, suggest what sort of company you are and be memorable.

Step 1: Brainstorm

Start by brainstorming for ideas. Write down words and phrases that describe your business or have meaning for you. Business names often contain a person's name, a place name, or something that reflects the type of business you are running.

While brain storming, keep the following in mind:

- You need to stand out from the crowd; your name doesn't have to be the most amazingly imaginative phrase ever invented, but it does have to be different enough so you aren't confused with other businesses. Sometimes simple is all you need 'Mike's Dog Home Boarding Service' isn't going to win a prize for innovation but it's likely to be remembered by clients and is easily passed on by word of mouth.
- Using a place name has both positives and negatives. Boarders are generally localised businesses so it can help position you in your local market. However, if you think you may move in future and want to continue your business elsewhere or you want to expand to cover more areas a location-based name can be limiting. Places can also be descriptive; you might use your house name, or something that reflects your general location rather than an actual place name.
- Try to convey something about the service you offer – that it's run by you, that it's a service for dogs or that you offer boarding. Although if you plan to offer multiple services make sure your name reflects that.
- Think about what you want your name to say about you – caring, professional, fun, safe, funny, cute, friendly – how do you want your business to be perceived?

Step 2: Cross out any names that break these rules

Once you've got your initial list, narrow it down by crossing out any ideas that definitely won't work. Here are some rules that you should think twice about before breaking:

- Don't be too obscure; make sure people can pronounce your business name and relate it to dog care. A phrase that is very meaningful for you might not have the same meaning to other people.
- Avoid deliberate misspellings such as swapping an s for a z. If someone recommends your company while walking their dog in the park they are going to guess the spelling incorrectly. Particularly avoid doing it in an attempt to make yourself different from a similarly (but correctly spelt) company. You'll just create confusion and may end up sending customers to another business.
- Mashing words together or making up new ones can be counterproductive in a world where people search online to find services.
- If you use a pet's name that doesn't clearly belong to a dog, be prepared for people to think it's your name. Someone who's never met you before won't know that 'Bob's Dog Boarding' refers to a boarding service run by Mike who

WORKSHEET

About Your Business

Use this worksheet to help you provide a consistent message when you are marketing your business to dog owners.

Branding	
Business Name:	Logo:
Tag Line:	
Contact Information	
Telephone:	Colours:
Email:	
Website:	Fonts:
Social media:	

What you Offer
Describe your business in 100 words or less:

List 3 things that make your business unique from your competitors:	What key points should people know about your service? This should include where you are and what you offer.
•	•
•	•
•	•
	•

has a dog called Bob. If you use a pet's name also consider how you'd feel if they passed away.

- It used to be that business directories were organised alphabetically, hence the number of business names like A1, AA and even AAA. Now business searches are carried out online there is no benefit to this naming convention.

- Be careful of phrases that may be offensive or misconstrued, bad puns, foreign words or local dialect. You'll need to be able to say the name with a straight face in polite company.

- If you don't have the marketing budget of Apple, then pick a name that conveys the service you offer.

- Check for common names used in similar local businesses and try to avoid them, e.g. whiskers, paws, wagging, pooch.

- Make sure you don't use trademarks in your name, such as cartoon characters or advertising catch phrases. Trademark holders actively hunt down people using their trademark in order to protect their rights. To check if something is trademarked go to: www.ipo.gov.uk/tmtext/

Step 3: Check not already in use

Once you have a shortlist you need to check there is no one operating with a similar name. There are thousands of home boarders operating in the UK, and even more worldwide, so many names are already in use. You might think you've come up with a unique and original business name, but it's important to double check. To do that:

- Check Companies House for any companies with that name. This only includes registered companies, not small businesses that operate as self-employed sole traders.

- Search online for the name to see if anyone else is using it; also check for similarly named businesses that are operating in the same area as you.

- If you plan to have a website, you might like to check if a domain name is available that matches the business name.

Step 4: Run your final ideas past other people

By now you should have just a couple of names or variations and it's time to try them out. Show the names to people, preferably those in your target audience, and get their opinions. This will help make sure it does say what you planned about your business and that there aren't any negative connotations associated with it. Sometimes what you think is a great play on words or a memorable name might not work for other people. Surveying people that you don't know well may help you get more honest responses.

Rather than just asking "Do you like this name?" try asking questions like:

- What sort of business do you think would have a name like that?
- What service do you think a business with that name offers?
- What do you think of when you hear this name?
- Tell them the name, and ask the next day if they can remember it.
- Tell them the name, and ask how they'd spell it.

Make sure you listen to what your target audience tells you. Don't get so attached to a name that you stick with it when your research is showing that it won't work well for you. Your name will represent your business for many years so take the time to get it right, even if it means going back to the brainstorming stage and starting again.

Reaching Your Potential Clients

After completing your market analysis you should have a good idea of who your clients are going to be and what they want, so now you need to work out where and how you will make contact with them. There are two aspects to this: you want to make sure people currently looking for boarding find your details, but you also want to generally raise awareness that your service exists among your target market so they remember you if they need boarding in future.

Start by brainstorming ideas for where your target market might look for boarding providers, see advertising or go to for advice on dog-related issues.

Places people in your target market might try to find details of boarders include the following:

- Business directories (both online and paper)
- Online search engines
- Local internet groups
- Asking their vet, local pet shop or groomer for recommendations
- Asking other dog owners for recommendations

The places people in your target market generally hang out, read information or people they talk with might include the following:

- Vet practices, groomers and pet shops
- Local events like fêtes or open days
- Local papers or newsletters

- Local shops, parks and recreation areas

It's important that you think very specifically about your target audience; don't assume all dog owners will go to the same places and read the same websites. For example:

- If you are targeting people looking for budget dog boarding, they are likely to also be using local pet shops that market themselves as low cost options or offer frequent discounts rather than an expensive boutique pet shop.
- If your target customers live in a small local area then a national newspaper is unlikely to be cost effective, but a local paper or newsletter might work well.
- If your target demographic is over 65 years old they are less likely to use the internet to find information than those under 40 years old.

Being specific will help you target locations where your potential clients will see the advert and avoid wasting time and money on marketing to people that aren't going to use your service.

Don't just rely on where *you* think people will go. Ask people, particularly the people you are targeting. Friends, family, and existing clients may all have helpful ideas you hadn't thought of. You can refine your advertising locations over time by looking at the response you get from each area.

Once you've identified some places that your target customers visit or use for information, you'll need to think about how you can make sure your business is promoted in those locations. For example, if you think your local vet practice will be a good location you need to decide if business cards, posters, the practice newsletter or recommendations from the staff would work best to share your message.

Adverts

There are lots of locations you can place adverts including local papers, business directories, shop windows or websites. The cost of advertising will vary a lot, and some adverts can be very expensive. Make sure you ask questions about how many people will see them, how long the advert will be displayed and how much it will cost before you commit. Think about how many people are likely to see and respond to your advert and how much that will translate to in terms of cost per booking.

You'll need to tailor your adverts to the place you are advertising but here are some general tips to keep in mind when creating an advert.

- Make sure it's clear what service you are offering. If your business name describes your service. For example 'Mel's Dog Boarding', then that may be all you need. Otherwise add a tag line such as "Dog Boarding" or "Holiday Care for Dogs".

- The most important part of an advert is instructing people what to do if they are interested in your services. Make sure your contact information is easy to find and easy to read (don't use tiny text).

- Find out if there are any constraints such as size or colour before you design your advert, and whether the place you are advertising will help you out with formatting.

- Be honest and specific on your advert. Adverts that are misleading can land you in legal trouble. If you only take small dogs then state that on your advert. Generating lots of calls doesn't help if the customers are unsuitable – it just wastes your time and theirs.

- Make sure your adverts look professional: do not use all capital letters, make sure to leave gaps around text and images, and only use one or two different fonts – do not go crazy, stick to your branding.

- Think about three key points you want to make and don't try to tell people everything about your service in one advert.

- If you are including photographs get written permission from the owners of the dogs in them. Don't use stock photos or photos you've found online of dogs to illustrate your adverts. If you aren't good at taking photos then ask a friend or relative to help out, or even ask your clients if they have any photos of their dogs that you could use.

- The final step for every advert is to proofread it. Get someone else to do this for you as it's easy to miss your own errors. Look for misspellings, poor grammar, accidently cut off words, the wrong phone number and typos in your email address.

Posters

Before going to the time and expense of designing and printing posters make sure you have permission to put them up where you plan. In general you can't put up posters advertising your business on lampposts, bus stops, the park or even your garden gate. If you aren't sure ask your local council what the rules are for your area. You may be able to put posters up inside buildings such as on a vet's notice board, but you'll need permission from the owner first, and check if they have a size limit.

Vehicle signs

If you use a car or van in the course of your work then you can turn it into a moving advert for your services by adding graphics to the side panels. It can be a good way to put advertising in places you wouldn't be able to put posters e.g. the car park of the local popular dog walking spot, so you get your message right in front of the people that are most likely to use your services. Car signs can either be vinyl (a sticker) or magnetic. Magnetic signs are handy if you don't want the advert on your car all of the time.

Business Cards and Leaflets

Printed information about your business such as business cards, leaflets, and postcards are useful when you want to give potential clients information about yourself.

Business cards are a handy and professional way to give someone your contact information. It's a good idea to carry a few cards with you all the time; you never know when you might meet someone that needs boarding. Your business card should have your name, business name, phone number, and, if you use them, email, website, and social media accounts. Make it easy to read and match it to your branding with your logo or colour scheme. If you have space you could add a sentence or bullet points highlighting key information about your service.

Leaflets should have the same contact information as a business card but give you more opportunity to include details about your service, photos and information such as prices. You could also consider posting leaflets or postcards through doors in the area your target users live or even a letter to tell them about the business you are starting. Make sure you check with your local council whether there are any regulations you need to follow when distributing leaflets.

In today's high tech world, how you use printed business literature will be linked with how you and your target market use the internet. If you have a website and your target market uses the internet, you may just use a business card to direct people to your website. If your target market doesn't go online much, then leaflets may be an important way for you to provide more in depth written information about your business.

Many companies offer printing for small numbers of cards or leaflets e.g. 50, 100 or 250. Although the prices per item will lower the more you order don't be tempted to buy too many at once in the first go. That way you can see how many you use, check the design and won't be stuck with lots spare if you decide to make any amendments later. You could also print your own; you can buy business cards on an A4 sheet that will go through most home printers so you can just print what you need as you go. You'll need to weigh up which option gives you the correct balance of expense and professionalism.

Press Releases

Press releases are statements sent to newspapers, magazines, websites, blogs and newsletter editors with information about something newsworthy you are doing in the hope that they'll publish the details. A press release should contain the following:

- Your name and contact details
- Facts about you, such as your business name, start-up date, brief summary
- One or two photos

What marketing works for your business?

"I have a Facebook page, a website, my car is wrapped with my business name etc but by far the most important and effective way of business promotion is WORD OF MOUTH. Anyone that has a dog knows that dog walkers tend to talk to other dog walkers so once you find somewhere you like and trust you will tell everyone you meet! "

- Hayley Elliott-Edwards, Scruffy Mutts

"I've found the best way of marketing for me is the Find Pet Boarding website, most of my business comes from there. I also have a Facebook page, which I advertise on different sites and occasionally pay Facebook for advertising. I have paid for an active website but I have found my clients mainly come through Find Pet Boarding and Facebook, and now word of mouth, with plenty of client references. When I first started the business I had leaflets made, business cards and car advertising, for me this didn't work! Leaflet drops don't work as they get thrown away amongst other leaflets. I have left leaflets in vets/pet shops but again this didn't work for me. "

- Claire Harper, Your Pet Pal

"Try and work with anyone that boards/walks in your area by passing on clients to each other. "

- Katherine White, Happy Pawz home dog boarding

- A statement that you can be contacted for more information or photos
- The story you are sharing. Write in third person (as if you are writing about someone else), but include quotes in your own words. Write about 300–400 words in total.

It's important that the story you are trying to share is interesting or entertaining. The goals of newspapers and other news sharing sources are different from yours – they aren't promoting your business, they are looking for stories that their readers will want to hear.

For a small local paper a new business or expansion might be enough to be interesting, but you should still try to standout. Imagine there are several different boarders starting out and they can only cover one – why is your story the most interesting? Later on you might tell a story about the strangest boarding guest you've had, a cause or campaign, an achievement (gaining a qualification or the first year of business), or you may share your opinion or reaction to something topical, such as the council changing dog walking laws or a local event like a dog show.

To be valuable as a marketing tool, your press release needs to be published somewhere your target market will read it, so think about local organisations that put out newsletters that might reach dog owners, such as vets, pet shops, and local event guides.

Word of Mouth

Many boarding clients come through word of mouth: someone telling someone else about your service. Word of mouth is one of the best forms of marketing because it involves personal recommendations and those carry a lot of weight for people who are choosing a boarding service.

Some word-of-mouth marketing will occur naturally; if your clients like your service they will recommend you to someone else they know who is looking for boarding. The more people who know about your service and talk to others about it, the more your message will spread. You can help this along by making sure as many people know about you as possible. Tell your friends and family about your new business; even if they don't have a dog they may have friends or colleges with one and be able to mention you if the topic of dogs or holidays comes up. You could also encourage people to refer people to your service by offering an incentive such as a free day's boarding for each friend they refer.

Business networking
Word-of-mouth recommendation can also come from other businesses. You can encourage this to happen by networking with other businesses that share your target market. Introduce

yourself to other businesses at networking events and look for opportunities to mix with people from other local pet businesses at dog-related events such pet shows or rescue open days. Look out for influencers, people who are in a position to talk to dog owners such as pet shop staff, vet receptionists or rescue centre home checkers. You'll need to register with a vet practice as a condition of your boarding licence, so try picking a quiet period and going in person to meet the staff and let them know about your business.

When you talk to people, be careful not come across as just there to promote yourself. While many people don't mind a chat, they won't want to listen to an advertising spiel about your business. Mention it casually or when you introduce yourself, and leave it at that unless you are prompted for more information. Make sure you ask them about their business too, you may even get tips on marketing from people with experience at reaching your target market. Once you get to know other local business owners you'll be able to make referrals back in return – make a point of knowing the best vet, groomer, pet shop or cattery in town and recommend them to people. Networking is about mutual benefit so you offer support to other businesses and receive some in return.

Networking can involve other boarders too. Although other dog boarders might be in competition with you for bookings; working with them can actually benefit both of your businesses. Your 'competition' can also provide backup in emergencies, somewhere to refer people when you are booked up or a source of advice and support for dealing with problems so you can offer a higher standard of service and attract more clients.

Positive attention given to home boarding generally can also benefit all home boarders in the area. Imagine a competitor puts an advert in the local paper – someone reads about boarding who hasn't heard about this sort of service before. They call your competitor but find they are fully booked so they start looking for other boarders in the area and find your service. You've benefited from the marketing that your competitor has done. You can make that benefit even more effective if you work with other boarders to promote home boarding as an option and refer clients between you if you have an enquiry from someone you can't help. If you find out that someone has referred a client to you, make sure you take time to thank them.

Online Marketing

The internet offers a wide range of ways to market your business including a website of your own, social media channels, directories and search engines.

Don't feel you have to have a website to have an online presence. Many dog boarders use other platforms such as social media or business directories to make their business findable online.

Of course, there is no rule that you have to be online at all; you may decide that you can successfully market your business in more traditional ways.

It's important that the reason you choose marketing options is because after careful research you've decided they will work for your business, not just because someone says 'you should have a website'.

Business website

A website can be a useful way for you to share information about your business and the services you offer. A website acts like a brochure on the internet; it can accommodate a lot of information, including videos and photos, and it's easier to change than printed materials. Websites don't need to be complicated, just a few pages such as:

- About you – including why you started the business, your qualifications and experience.
- Services – to explain what you offer and how much it costs; you might also include frequent questions or explain your policies on what dogs you accept.
- Contact Information – to include your contact phone and emails and your location. You might also like to add contact information to the header and footer of every page as it's essential that it should be easy to find.

Other information you might include could be a gallery showing your facilities and walks, reviews from past clients and updates on your business.

The cost of a website varies a great deal. Free options are available that provide a basic template in which you can change the text and images. Professional websites can be expensive, although they'll be more customised to your business and a good website development company will also offer advice on how to make sure people find your website and make it easy to use. If you're lucky you may know someone who can help you put something simple together. You may want to consider starting out with a free or template website to see if it works for your business before paying a large amount.

You'll need to think about how people in your target market will find out about your website. You might include your website's address on your other adverts or business cards and encourage people to visit for more information. If you'd like your website to be listed in search engines like Google this takes a little more work as you'll be competing with everyone else to be first in the search results. Be wary of companies that offer to get you a 'number one spot in Google'. They can't guarantee search engine results unless you pay for advertising.

Tips on websites

- Think carefully about what information you share online, for you and your client's privacy.
- Avoid clip art, animations and stock photos. If you do use any images you find online, you must have permission. Where possible use your own images as they can represent your business the best.
- Shop around and get quotes if you employ a company to build your website. Make sure the amount you spend is appropriate for the amount of business it's likely to generate.

How do you use social media to help your business?

"We use Facebook to keep in touch with owners privately and to post photos publicly, which people like to follow."

- Bev Halstead, Ffoslas Farm Pet Hotel

"I have two Facebook accounts relating to my business - my business one, and then an additional one which is a secret group and only customers with dogs in get access to this and this is where they log in to it and each dog has its own separate album. I also post daily updates on it, I never place home board dogs on my business profile so then it protects the safety of the dogs - just due to all the dog thefts etc. We also have a Twitter account and I am just starting a Youtube one as well."

- Lisa Clark, Birtle Home Boarding

"I have a Facebook group and when I first started I asked my friends and family to add any of their friends and family who owned dogs. I also join local business advertising groups and posted on them. I asked different local business if I could put a post on their business page in return they could put a post on mine. I changed my profile picture to my business photo and had my phone number/email on it."

- Katherine White, Happy Pawz home dog boarding

- Make sure your website matches your other advertising, so use colours, font styles and your logo. Most templates allow you to make basic changes.
- Make sure your contact information is prominent and can be found on or from every page.
- Think about how regularly you can commit to updating the information, don't include a news page if you won't have the time or budget to update it regularly. A news page that hasn't been updated in a year will make people wonder if your business is no longer trading.
- Think about the different ways people access the internet: your website will need to work for desktop, mobile, and tablet users so try it from different devices.
- Think about the questions clients regularly ask; adding information on these topics can save you time answering calls and replying to emails.
- Search engines use the text on your website to decide what it's about and whether it contains the information someone is searching for. Make sure your website's text contains all the key information about you including the names of the towns or areas you cover and the services you offer.

Online directories

Business directories can offer an alternative to having your own website. They are an online version of the telephone directory with lists of businesses by type or area. They often allow you a dedicated page that you can use to provide information and photos of your business. There are general directories such as Yellow Pages and those dedicated to boarding such as Find Pet Boarding. Directories can work well because they'll do the marketing for you, attracting visitors to their site who will then be directed to your advert.

As with a website, they work best when you take the time to add information and photos so people can see what your business offers.

Social media

Social media platforms encourage users to network and share information with each other. Examples include Facebook, Twitter and Instagram. Social media can be a useful tool to connect with new clients, but also to maintain a relationship with existing clients. Many home boarders use social media to share information and photos about walks and update clients on their dog's stay.

Facebook offers 'business pages' specifically designed to allow businesses to share information about and communicate with clients. Social media is about making connections and networking, not directly promoting yourself. Use it as a tool to update current clients, advice on pet care, topical issues and what's happening with your business. Try to post regularly even if it's not very often – once a month is fine.

Social media can also include community groups, such as ones for local businesses or dog owners which may be a good opportunity to advertise – always check community rules first to make sure you are allowed to self-promote.

It's important to remember that what you share online can be impossible to take back, so you must always conduct yourself professionally. If your business page is linked to your personal accounts make sure they also reflect well on you and avoid posting anything that may be off-putting to people who don't share your views.

Online reviews

Many people will use the internet to check what other people think of businesses before using their service. Encouraging clients to leave online reviews after using your service is a great tool to promote your service to future clients. Some clients will leave reviews without being asked, but it's also helpful to suggest it and direct people to places where they can leave a review.

Positive reviews are an excellent marketing tool, but many business worry about receiving negative reviews. Keep in mind that even the best of businesses sometimes get negative or unfavourable reviews. Studies have shown people can even be suspicious about the credibility of reviews if a business only has positive ones. So while they can be a worry, a single negative review is not the end of the world.

It's natural to be upset when someone leaves an unfavourable comment about your business, but the important thing is how you respond to negative comment. Many sites will give you the opportunity to rebut reviews and a great response to a negative review can leave people with a good impression of your service and carry more weight than the original comment. Think of a negative review as an opportunity to demonstrate that you listen to your clients and work hard to resolve problems. As a consumer yourself, you'll know sometimes you run into problems with a service or product, and how the company reacts to resolve the problem will determine how you feel about them and whether you use their service again in future. If a company responds swiftly and helpfully, you'll be left with a positive impression, even if your original experience didn't go smoothly.

When you reply to a negative review, bite your tongue and be nice. Make sure your tone is polite and thank the reviewer for taking the time to leave a comment. Sometimes the best option is to just acknowledge they feel there is a problem and say you'll contact them privately to work it out. If the reviewer raises issues that you can resolve, contact them to do so – but be polite and don't express anger at the fact they left a review. Some reviewers find it difficult to raise issues face to face, so they might not have been confident about telling you the problem even if you could have easily resolved it. After you've addressed the problem, they may be happy to go back and alter the review.

If you find you get more than the very occasional negative comment you may need to look at your business practices to see what is causing the recurring problem.

Your Existing Clients

Marketing is not just about getting new clients. Existing clients are your most valuable resource – it's much easier to retain clients than find new ones. This means that keeping your clients happy and coming back should be something you actively focus on doing.

Although you are just starting and won't have existing clients, you might like to think about how you will retain them as you build your business. For clients who take annual holidays, it may be a year between contact, so simply reminding them that you are there and how to book can help maintain a relationship. This can be done in various ways including email newsletters, asking them to follow your Facebook page, sending birthday or Christmas cards or dropping them a note when they usually book to remind them to reserve their place. If you know a client usually holidays the same time each year you might like to call them a few months in advance and check if they'd like to reserve that period. You could also offer incentives such as a discount for regular bookings or a loyalty discount, such as a free day for every ten days they book.

Monitoring Your Marketing

One of the most important things about marketing is to monitor how well it works. Marketing is something you'll be doing on an ongoing basis so you can refine it over time to make it more effective. You need to know which types of marketing bring you the most enquiries. Advertising in the newspaper may be worthwhile if it generates lots of enquiries but if you do not get any enquires, you know not to spend money on it in future.

To learn about the effectiveness of your marketing you need to keep track of how every potential client who contacts you found out about your business. The simplest way to do this is to ask them where they heard of you. You can note this information down and see over time where your clients come from. Online marketing can be easier to track as websites keep electronic records of how many people view them and how they reached them. If you have your own website you should use monitoring tools to keep track of this, and if you place adverts on other websites, ask them to share the information with you. This will let you know how many people access the information you've put up and you can compare this with how many people go on to make an enquiry to see how effective your marketing is.

Monitoring your results isn't just about where you advertise; it can also be used to refine how you advertise. If you put up a poster in your local vets but no one ever claims that's where they saw your details then you might decide it's not worth paying to have a poster there. Or you might decide instead to try a different poster to see if changing the design or information will make it work better.

WORKSHEET

Marketing Plan

Use this worksheet to plan the how you will market your business and think about how the methods you have chosen will help you achieve your goals. Make sure you keep track of you results.

	Activity 1	Activity 2
What are you going to do? E.g. posters in local pet shops		
Who are you targeting? Be specific!		
Why have you chosen this method?		
What will it cost?		
What do you need to do to implement this?		
When will you do this?		
What's you goal? E.g. To get five bookings or to raise general awareness		
How well did it work?		

10

Taking Bookings

Having run a successful marketing campaign, your phone is, hopefully, buzzing with potential clients. Don't relax yet though, you still have to convert these potential clients into paying ones.

Initial Enquiries

When a potential client calls or emails, the first thing to ascertain is whether you have space for the period they want to book and whether you can meet their dog's needs.

Answering the phone

Make sure you, and any other family members, always answer the phone politely, as you never know when it may be a potential client calling.

Think about how you will answer – "Hello, Mel's Dog Boarding" gives a better first impression than a gruff "Hello". Smile when you answer the phone, it will come across in your voice. It may be helpful to have a quiet space for a phone conversation, an office or spare room so you can shut a door between barking dogs, children and other family members. Make sure family know not to interrupt while you are talking to clients. If you dread answering calls and get flustered, ask someone to help you practise. Get them to make up a dog and a holiday, and go through the questions you would ask a real prospective client.

Have rules about when you will answer the phone and when you'll leave it to go to voice mail. If you are boarding a dog that reacts badly to the phone ringing then turn the volume down, use a mobile on vibrate or send calls to voice mail and call back. Don't answer calls while dog walking, you need your full attention on the dog and you won't have information you need to hand. Likewise don't answer the phone while driving, even with a hands-free kit; you need to be able to give the prospective client your full attention. You may also want to think about setting business hours to make sure you keep a good work-life balance. If the advertising medium allows, include a best time to call and an explanation for why they may get voice mail, i.e. you're busy focusing on the dogs in your care but you'll call them back.

Have a clear and friendly message ready for when a call goes to voice mail that encourages people to leave a message. If you have a dedicated business line, then use a message that lets the prospective client know they've reached the right number, for example:

> *Hello, you've reached Mel's Dog Boarding service. Sorry I can't answer your call at the moment but please leave your name and phone number and I will call you back.*

If other people may be taking a message for you then have a pad by the phone for them to write on and make sure they are clear on what information they need to record. It's also a good idea to be clear on what, if any, information you'd like them to give out – for example, you don't want them to quote your fees incorrectly.

Answering emails

Email enquiries are easier to deal with as you have the luxury of more time to think about what you want to say. You still need to reply to messages promptly though, as the prospective client may contact several boarders and may choose someone else if you delay too long. That said, you should still manage your business and personal time so you aren't spending all your spare time checking for messages. Generally replying to morning messages by the end of the day, and afternoon/evening messages the next morning will be considered reasonable. It may help to have template emails ready to reply to standard questions, so you don't have to type similar replies over and over again, such as an email that explains your standard terms that you can just edit slightly to confirm dates each time.

Emails can also be a useful follow up to phone calls to confirm information in writing for both you and the clients benefit. That way you've got a record of what was agreed in case there is any disagreement later.

It's possible to set up automatic replies, in other words an email that is sent out automatically whenever you are sent a message. You don't need a permanent automatic reply. However, they can be useful if you are particularly busy or away for a few days to acknowledge the email and explain there will be a delay in your response. If you do use an auto reply, make sure it's up to date – sending an auto reply that says you're currently unavailable with dates six months old make it look like you are unorganised or may even have stopped trading.

Exchanging information

Generally people call or email with a specific date in mind they need boarding for, so one of the first things to ascertain is if you have space for that date. If you don't then it doesn't matter how wonderful their dog is or they think you are, you probably won't be taking a booking. You'll also want to check their dog is suitable for your home boarding service. You might ask questions such as:

- Has the dog ever shown aggression towards people? Be wary about a slight nip written off as not a problem – remember you'll be responsible if the dog bites someone while in your care.
- Has the dog ever shown aggression towards other dogs? If so, what were the circumstances. It might be possible to accommodate this if you only take one dog and don't have resident dogs. However, you'll have to think carefully about how you will manage walks.
- Do they have any other behavioural issues – barking, urinating in the house, shredding soft furnishing or hating car travel?
- Check that their dogs fit with any policies you have on the type of dogs you'll care for, such as size, breed, neuter status or sociability with other dogs.

If you can't accommodate the dates they want or their dog, if possible try to help them anyway; it's handy to have the numbers of other local boarders you feel comfortable recommending to pass on. You may find they'll remember you were helpful next time they are looking for boarding and the other boarders in the area may return the favour if they have someone they can't help.

If you think that you could provide the boarding they need, then the key information to give out during the first call or email is:

- A summary of what you'll provide as part of the service. Keep in mind they may not have used a home boarding service before.
- Your prices, the payment terms, the amount the deposit will be and the cancellation terms. It's a good idea to record the price you quote them.
- Your address, so they know where to come for the pre-stay meeting, and a contact phone or email if they don't have it.

If possible, send the prospective client copies of your full terms and conditions and contract. If they've phoned, ask for an email address to send them to. If they don't have one, you could post them out if there is time for them to arrive before you plan to meet the owners. If not, summarise the key points for them over the phone.

Key information to get from the prospective client:

- Their name and their dog's name.
- A contact number in case you need to get in touch with them. For example, you may have to reschedule a meeting because of an unexpected vet trip.
- The dates they want to book. At this stage it's a good idea to mark the dates as provisionally booked on your availability calendar.

You might find it helpful to have a written list of questions to ask or topics to cover next to the phone so you can easily remember all the points you need to make and what you need to ask. It can also help to make a brief note of anything a prospective client asks about, such as outside facilities, so you can discuss these points further when you meet them.

Once you have answered their questions, if they are still interested in your services, arrange for a meeting date, and don't forget to tell them how to get to you.

Meeting Prospective Clients

Sometimes potential clients will be ready to book before they've even met you; others may visit more than one boarding provider before making up their minds. Generally it's best to meet a client and their dog at least once before confirming a booking. That way you can check that the dog is 'as described' and make sure they understand the terms and conditions of boarding. If you don't meet the dog, you should have a plan for what to do if a client turns up to drop off their dog and you find that the information they've given isn't quite accurate – perhaps the dog is badly matted, got fleas or is nervous of you and the owners want to drop him off to catch a flight in a couple of hours.

When meeting prospective clients, you need to make sure that their dog is a good fit for your boarding service. You also need to demonstrate to the client that you will provide a safe and enjoyable option for their dog boarding needs. Be organised and plan what you'll do during the meeting; for example, you might start with a tour of your home and then move on to discussing their dog's requirements and filling out paperwork. It can be helpful to have a written list of what information you need to go through, particularly the first few times you meet prospective clients.

Do you have any advice for taking bookings?

"Think about how you answer the phone. I have called boarders and had the phone answered by their young child as dogs bark loudly in the background - it does not give the impression of a professional service that the boarder has under control. "

- Tamsin Stone, Find Pet Boarding

"When a client makes contact, I take initial basic information for example age/sex/breed/neutered or spayed and what the client requires, then I have a much more in-depth boarding agreement form which the client has to fill out prior to us meeting or bring it to me on the initial meeting so that we can go through it together. I then meet them to make sure all is good."

- Claire Harper, Your Pet Pal

"Before taking on any dog they have to come over for a familiarisation visit so I can see how their dog is, meet my two and they can see where their dog will be staying. I'll give them a form to take away and fill in before their dog stays so they can tell me exactly their dogs likes/dislikes/routine. I emphasise how important it is and customers then realise how much I care. "

- Kim Knowles, Bertie & Shelby's Home from Home Holiday

"Relax! They are often quite nervous about leaving their pets with you (ALWAYS have a prelim meeting). Welcome them into your home, show them the garden, and explain which rooms their pet will have access/sleep in. Discuss diet, exercise, funny habits, phobias, they will gladly tell you all about their furbaby. If they want to book a stay I go through a registration form with them and always take a small nonreturnable deposit. They should bring their dog(s) to meet you/your dog(s). I usually close off the upstairs and carpeted living room - dogs will often want to leave their mark so encourage them to go into your garden to relieve themselves. It's probably easier if there are no other visiting dogs in your home at the time. "

- Carole Morgan, Chez Jasper

Generally clients will be looking for a boarder who has good personal qualities as well as professionalism, they will want to leave their dog with someone they 'feel' they can trust. First impressions are very important; after all they are proposing to leave a member of their family with someone who is almost a complete stranger. Give a professional impression: yes, you'll probably have some dog hair but try to avoid actual holes in walls or looking like you've just rolled around in mud with dogs (unless you think your clients will consider that a bonus).

Most people will want to see where their dog will be living so show them the areas where their dog will eat, sleep and play, both indoors and outdoors, so they can see they are clean and safe. In the garden, you might point out the space for running around and the toys you keep to hand. And indoors you might show them the quiet area where dogs can go to sleep and get away from the bustle of pack life if they want some time to themselves.

Some clients may have difficulties asking questions or not be sure what they should be asking so you might have to lead the discussion. They may find it helpful to know things like how long you've been boarding, what experience you have with dogs, and the qualifications you have, for example canine first aid. If they haven't used a home boarder before you might need to explain more generally what the service includes and how it differs from a kennel. The meeting is also an opportunity to ask them questions about their dog including the requirements for exercise, diet, where and when they like to sleep and any behavioural or medical issues, to make sure you can accommodate their needs.

Taking a Booking

At the end of the meeting your prospective clients may be ready to book and you can either go through the dog information form and boarding agreement to finalise the booking there and then or give them a copy to take away and fill in. Some prospective clients may visit other boarders or want to go home and "think about it" before booking. Don't be upset if that's the case, just thank them for coming and give them a business card with your contact details in case they think of anything else they would like to know.

If you provided a copy of your dog information form in advance and the owners have filled out or they return the form later, still take time to talk through it with them. This gives them the opportunity to think of additional information to add and you can clarify points you need to with them. Make sure you write everything down; never rely on remembering what you've been told.

Make sure clients have a written copy of your terms and conditions and that they sign to confirm they have read them. It's helpful to run through them and check they don't have any questions. It's much better to make clients aware of your terms for cancellation, for example, ahead of time, rather than encountering a problem and then having to point out what they agreed to as they didn't bother to read them. If they are ready to book, then get them to sign any permission forms and the boarding agreement, otherwise give them copies to take away to return when they are ready.

Booking confirmation

It's a good idea to confirm any verbally agreed booking in writing, either via email or in the post. Include the dates or the booking, the total cost and any key dates for payments, such as when the deposit and balancing payment are due. If there is any dispute about what information you gave or a miscommunication about dates, having the information in writing will prove invaluable.

Along with the booking confirmation, provide any other information the client may need such as a checklist of what to bring on the day of boarding.

Payment

Make sure you've decided at what point in the booking you want payment and that you get it before proceeding. Don't make exceptions just because the owner seems lovely. It's tough to turn down a client but if you know payment is an issue it's something you'll have to do.

Payment methods

Ten years ago small businesses dealt almost exclusively in cash and cheques. Now there are a wide range of other payment options, including:

- Online bank transfer
- PayPal (a website for sending/receiving payments online)
- A card reading device linked to your mobile phone (processes face to face payments)
- Card payment machine
- Merchant account and online payment gateway

The ability for your clients to make card payments can make it more convenient for them to pay, but processing cards involves a charge. Depending on the service this may be a fixed amount per transaction, or a percentage of the payment. You'll need to weigh up the pros and cons of card payments and, if you do accept them, factor in the costs when you set your prices.

It's worth noting that some pet insurance includes cover for emergency boarding fees, for example if the owner is hospitalised or delayed on holiday. Not all owners notice this term so if you board a dog in this type of circumstance suggest the owner checks their insurance, as they may be pleasantly surprised to find your fees will be reimbursed. They'll usually need you to provide a receipt to make a claim.

Haggling

From time to time you may come across clients who want to haggle over your prices. Presuming you've carefully calculated what prices are appropriate for your area and what you need to earn to make a living, don't be bullied into changing your rates. If they quote somewhere they can get care cheaper – you have to wonder why they aren't using that service, it may well be because they are fully booked or they aren't as good. Remember you don't have to take their business and they don't have to use your service. That they want to haggle already means they want your service – so stand firm. If you offer a discount this time, they are likely to want it again and may tell their friends.

This is one of the reasons researching prices in your area so that you price yourself appropriately is important; at some point someone will tell you your service is too expensive and it will give you the confidence to stick by your prices.

Pre-Stay Visits

In addition to a first meeting with the client and their dog, you may suggest further meetings such as a trial overnight stay or an afternoon settling-in session so the dog can get to know you better before being left for a full week or more on holiday. It can also be reassuring for the clients to have 'tested' your service and know their dog settles well in your care.

You should have the dog's information form and the signed boarding agreement before you provide any care – even for a short test stay. This is important as they give you the permissions and information required by your licensing conditions and make sure the owner agrees with your terms and conditions for providing care – for example, that they are responsible for the cost of vet care. If the boarding booking is subject to a successful test stay, the agreement should include a break clause that can be used if the test stay doesn't go well and either the client or you don't want to proceed with the booking.

If you plan to board dogs from different families or you have your own dog you will need to arrange a meeting for all the dogs that will be present during boarding so you can check they get along.

Turning Down Clients

It's likely at first, while you are getting established, that you'll be keen to snap up any clients that come your way. Don't automatically say yes to the first person who calls; not every prospective client will be suitable for your boarding service.

Be wary of people with very specific requirements you're not sure you can meet, who want to haggle over money, who you don't feel sure are being honest about their dog's behaviour, or who list all the things another boarder did wrong (which don't sound that terrible to you). Trust your instincts! A bad client can be stressful; and unless you have no possibility of filling the slot with someone else and need the income it may be worth letting the potential client go elsewhere.

It's also important to make it clear from the start that test stays are tests and you may not be able to go forward with the booking – don't get their hopes up by saying it's just a precaution.

What would make you turn down a booking?

"I'm quite specific, I'd rather not have a dog in, than take any dog just for money... and I don't want to upset my two! As after all it is our home too so it's got to be stress free! "

- Kim Knowles, Bertie & Shelby's Home from Home Holiday

"I don't generally take bookings from people that ring me late at night - it's usually an indication that they think I work 24 hours and they tend to be the ones that turn up late to pick up and drop off their dogs and don't respect that it's my home as well as my job. "

- Debbie Humphreys, Debbieduz Home Dog Boarding

"I would turn away a booking if I see any aggression, even slight lip lift baring teeth towards my dogs or my day dog. I'm also not happy to have dogs running along the top of my settees and jumping around on the furniture, without being asked. "

- Janie Wellman, The Wellmans Dog Home Boarding

Sometimes a dog will seem like a good fit when you discuss them with the client but the meeting doesn't go as you expect. Try to be non-confrontational and polite; for example, "Sorry I can't help but I think your dog would be happier somewhere else". Watch out for emotional blackmail, such as "If you don't take him little Rufus will have to stay in the scary kennels". You are running a business and it's the owner's responsibility to find care, not yours.

You may also want to turn a client down who wants to book short dates that don't fit well around other bookings. For example, a single day mid-week booking in peak holiday season would stop you taking a booking for the full week.

Whatever the reason you turn a client away, it's helpful to have a list of other boarding services that you can refer people to.

Being Turned Down

Not every prospective client will choose your boarding service. It can be quite disheartening to feel like someone doesn't like you. However, just because they didn't choose you it does not mean they thought you were a terrible boarder, it is just that they found a boarder more suited to their dog or situation. That may be as simple as the other boarder was cheaper, more experienced, had a dog that matched better with theirs or was just more convenient to get to. If someone does let you know they've chosen someone else, it is helpful to ask (politely) for the reason as feedback can help you improve your service; however, keep in mind they might not always give an accurate answer. If you find a lot of people call or visit but don't go on to use your service you need to have a good think about what may be putting them off.

Sometimes after a visit a prospective client may not contact you to let you know whether or not they want to use your services. Try not to take this too personally, they may have forgotten or just not bother to let you know, usually because they feel uncomfortable with telling you they have gone elsewhere. It's a good idea to have a set period you'll hold a provisional booking and let the prospective client know if you don't hear back by then you may take another client. Occasionally prospective clients may contact you months later for a booking because their situation has changed or their other boarding arrangements were not satisfactory so always be polite when people turn you down as they could still become clients in future.

11

Boarding Your First Dog

At last, after all that planning and hard work it's time to board your very first dog. If there is a reasonable gap between taking the booking and the stay itself, it may be helpful to contact the owner the week before the stay and check that everything is going to plan. You may want to:

- Remind them about any outstanding balance and check how they want to pay.
- Confirm anything they need to bring with their dog.
- Ask how their dog is and check there haven't been any changes to their health or new issues you need to be aware of.
- Arrange the time they plan to drop off their dog.

Drop Off

When the dog and their owner arrive make sure you have ready anything that still needs signing. You'll need to check the vaccination certificate they supply is up to date and covers the full boarding period. It's also a good idea to give the dog a once over and check their general condition – are they clean, a healthy weight, free from parasites and not showing any signs of illness?

Dogs arrive at boarding with a variety of luggage including food, treats, bedding, medication, collar and lead. Have somewhere prepared for storing food and other items the dog shouldn't have access to unsupervised. It can also be helpful to make an inventory of the dog's belongings so you can make sure they leave with everything they came with and there is no dispute over something the owner thought they brought but really forgot.

Allow plenty of time for the handover – dogs will be calmer and more relaxed if you and their owner are relaxed too, not rushing. Ask how the dog has been and if there is any final information you need to know. Check whether they've had any walks or mealtimes due already that day as the routine may have been upset by packing and travel to you.

Some owners may be nervous about leaving their dog, so it may help to offer to call or email them later in the day to let them know that their dog has settled. This is particularly the case if the dog has shown distress when they were leaving.

Settling In

Most dogs have great fun spending time with their home boarder and making new friends but many will also have some degree of anxiety at first about being left in a new place with a new person. One of your jobs will be to help them settle in as quickly and smoothly as possible to minimise any stress they feel. It's likely that the dog will be quite excited about the change in routine, so try and keep things low key on the first day – it's better to leave them to explore in

ASK A BOARDER

How do you help dogs settle in?

"I always insist on having a trial before accepting a new doggie into our home, as this enables us to get to know the dog before accepting a booking. It is also very important to find out the routine that they are used to, for example feeding times, exercise and sleeping arrangements. All these things will help them to settle in so much better. "

- Liz Knights, Oaklands Home Boarding

"I arrange for the family and the dogs to come and visit fill in paperwork and get all the information I can. If I feel or the owners ask I will do a half day visit or maybe two if needed. I ask the dogs owners to bring any that will help the dog settle in i.e. bed, toys, treats, crate. One even came with the owner's jumper! When the dog first arrives let them outside for a wee sometimes even before the owners have left. If the dog nervous when s/he first arrive I just sit on the floor and ignore the dog and let him/her come to me when ready. Then go for a walk a walk normally helps the dog settle down. If the dogs are ok when they first arrive we go out for a walk. "

- Katherine White, Happy Pawz home dog boarding

their own time rather than overwhelm them with cuddles and treats. For most dogs, sniffing your home and garden thoroughly will be the first thing on their agenda. Be guided by the dog's behaviour; some dogs will want to stick by your side and get plenty of reassurance and others will be more independent and want to investigate everything.

It may help to spend some time outside or take a few trips out to give them the opportunity to use the toilet after the excitement of a car journey, meeting you and saying goodbye to their owner. Going back to basics and rewarding a dog for toileting in an appropriate place will ensure they quickly get the idea of where to go while they stay with you.

Familiarity

Having familiar items such as their own bedding or toy can help a dog feel more at home. Scent is particularly important to dogs so their own bedding or an item of clothing with their owner's scent on can make it smell like home too. A DAP® (Dog Appeasing Pheromones) diffuser or spray can also provide a comforting scent that helps dogs to cope in stressful situations.

The benefits of short trial visits to get to know you and your home will show here; dogs that are already familiar with your home will settle more quickly. As you develop repeat customers you also find that dogs remember their previous stays, particularly if they had lots of fun activities, and settle back in quickly.

Routine

Maintaining a routine is one of the best ways to help a dog cope with the transition. Your dog information form and conversations with the owner should have given you a good feel for the dog's normal routine for feeding, walking and sleeping as well as little habits like having a treat before bedtime. Dogs will anticipate these events and find it reassuring that even in their new setting they can rely on resources, such as food, still turning up at the same time. Following a routine removes some of the uncertainty, which is a trigger for stress.

Expectations

Particularly at the start of the stay it's important that you keep your expectations reasonable. It will take dogs time to understand your house rules, and small things that you do differently such as where they eat meals or that you put your coat on after their lead whereas their owner does it the other way around. Even well-behaved and well-trained dogs may have an accident indoors or engage in some naughty attention-seeking behaviour when under stress. Settling in works both ways, it will also take you time to get used to an individual dog's quirks, such as how they signal they need a trip outside to toilet or ask to play.

Dog Welfare

While a dog is in your care you are responsible for their well-being, which means making sure their physical and emotional needs are met. There is no single "perfect" way to care for a dog; every dog is different and part of being a good boarder is the ability to adapt your care to each dog's needs. However, your care should always be underpinned by the five welfare needs identified by the Animal Welfare Act (see page 32).

Environment

You should have prepared your home to make it safe and comfortable for dogs, but this will be the true test of your house proofing; keep a close eye on dogs particularly for the first few days as they settle in. You may find you have a cushion-stealer or post-shredder, or that you have overlooked something in your preparations. To make sure you maintain a suitable environment, you'll need to keep on top of cleaning and make adjustments for the weather so the temperature stays comfortable.

Diet

Dogs have different nutritional needs depending on the age, sex, breed, activity levels and health. Sticking to a dog's normal diet is particularly important as sudden changes can cause digestive upset. Make sure that you have been provided enough food for the full stay and that, if the food isn't in the original packaging, you know which brand it is in case you do need to buy more.

Providing treats can be a good way to bond with a dog, but too many treats or treats they are unused to eating may make them unwell so don't be tempted to spoil them too much! Where you are caring for more than one dog or have a dog of your own, it's a sensible precaution to feed them separately to avoid issues with food guarding.

Normal behaviour

Dogs that don't have enough to do can become bored and frustrated so include plenty of opportunities for play, including a mix of toys and interactive games with you. Providing an appropriate outlet for normal behaviours like chewing will also help a dog relax (and reduce the risk of damage to your soft furnishings).

Regular walks are important to keep a dog fit, active and give them a mental workout. You should already know a dog's usual exercise routine from your dog information form.

Social

Dogs are social animals and need companionship to avoid feeling lonely. Some dogs do not cope well with being left and may become distressed even if left for short periods. Even those that are usually comfortable with being on their own sometimes may be less settled in the unfamiliar environment and more clingy than usual. This may mean you need to be very available particularly in the first few days, as just going upstairs or to a different room may trigger anxiety. Some dogs will want to snuggle up and others will just like to know that you are around. Some dogs find talk radio helpful as it sounds like people are nearby.

Social dogs often enjoy the new playmates they meet while boarding. However, it's important that all dogs have the opportunity and space to get away from each other for a while if they choose to. Where dogs have different energy levels it might be necessary to separate them for short periods to let them wind down and sleep in peace. This can particularly be the case for young dogs or ones that have the tendency to get over excited while playing and get over tired if not encouraged to take a break.

If you are boarding more than one dog or have a dog of your own you'll need to ensure there are enough resources to go around – that includes beds, toys, water bowls, food and cuddles. Monitor dogs closely for any signs of competitiveness or being excluded.

Health

Sometimes the stress of a change of setting can trigger health problems so keep a close eye out for any changes in behaviour or that may signal a problem. If you have any concerns, call your vet to discuss them. It's always better to err on the side of caution and get a dog checked out if you are at all worried about their health. Make sure you keep your records of any medication you give up to date.

Home Time

On the final day of a dog's stay keep up the same routine until they are collected; they won't know it's going home day so changing a routine again can be unsettling. Dogs will find their owners arriving after a period away – even if it's just one night – very exciting. Make sure the dog is secured while their owners come into your home so they can say hello in a safe space. Don't let them out of the front door to greet them. Give the dog and owner time to say hello to each other and calm down before discussing the stay.

Most owners will want to know what their dog got up to during their holiday with you. You might have provided this as updates while they were away; if not, give them a rundown of the highlights – fun walks, how they got along with other dogs, what games they enjoyed. Photos are a great way to show owners what their dog did and they often find it reassuring to see their dog looking relaxed and happy.

Pack up the dog's things ready and if you've used an inventory to record what items the dog brought with them get the owner to sign to confirm everything is received. You'll also need to return the vaccination certificate and remove your boarding identification tags from the dog's collar.

Improving Your Service

Finally, think about how the stay went and whether there is anything you can learn from it. As a new boarder it's likely your service and business practices will evolve overtime as you learn from your experiences. Was there anything you could have done differently to make the booking smoother or stay better? Also think about the things that went well so you can repeat them; perhaps you found a particular bit of information about a dog useful to have – if so, make a note to ask other clients the same in future.

Now all that's left to do is enjoy your new career as a professional dog boarder!

Do you have any final words of wisdom?

"Over time I've learnt a lot - allocated pick up and drop offs are a must. Also I always have a trial day with a dog before I commit to having it for any length of time - if I had a £ for every time I've heard "he's never done that before" I would be very wealthy! "

— Debbie Humphreys, Debbieduz Home Dog Boarding

"Having any business at home people think your 'open all hours' & can expect to call or pick up their dog any time of day/night so I've had to be quite strict which people do respect once told! "

— Kim Knowles, Bertie & Shelby's Home from Home Holiday

"Always go with your gut instinct and always take full payment in advance."

— Steph Drake, Total Pet Expert

"Make the most of the sunny days, they make up for weeks of rain and muddy feet everywhere"

— Bev Halstead, Ffoslas Farm Pet Hotel

"Keep at it. First few months you will probably be quiet and have some moments where you feel like packing it in. But keep plugging away advertising etc and you will get busy. I'm 6 months in and was slowly building up a client base then in the new year things have gone mad. I'm getting quite busy with enquiries every day it seems. "

— Mathew Godwin

Useful links

Code of Practice for the Welfare of Dogs:
www.gov.uk/government/publications/code-of-practice-for-the-welfare-of-dogs

Level 2 Diploma in Animal Care:
www.caw.ac.uk/course/level-2-diploma-in-animal-care-online-learning

Pet Industry Federation:
www.petcare.org.uk

Dogs Trust Factsheets:
https://www.dogstrust.org.uk/help-advice/factsheets-downloads/

HMRC:
www.gov.uk/working-for-yourself

Information Commissioner's Office Guide to Data Protection:
www.ico.org.uk/for-organisations/guide-to-data-protection

Government Legislation:
www.legislation.gov.uk

Online boarding licence application:
www.gov.uk/animal-boarding-establishment-licence

Disclosure Scotland:
www.mygov.scot/basic-disclosure/apply-for-basic-disclosure

AccessNI Criminal Record Checks:
www.nidirect.gov.uk/services/apply-online-basic-check

Find Pet Boarding:
www.findpetboarding.com

References

Daventry District Council (2015) 'The Public Spaces Protection Order'
https://www.daventrydc.gov.uk/EasysiteWeb/getresource.axd?AssetID=41197

Eden District Council (2013) 'Model Licence Conditions for the Home Boarding of Dogs'
https://www.eden.gov.uk/media/1300/model-licence-conditions-for-the-home-boarding-of-dogs.pdf

LACORS (2005) Licence Conditions for Home Boarding (Dogs)
http://democratic.bracknell-forest.gov.uk/documents/s56946/AnimalBoard Establishments - Home
Boarding of Dogs.pdf

LACORS (2009) 'LACORS Model Home Boarding Conditions Update and Clarification'
http://democracy.allerdale.gov.uk/documents/s91892/LACORS%20appendix%202.doc.pdf

PDSA (2016) 'PDSA Animal Wellbeing (PAW) Report'
https://www.pdsa.org.uk/get-involved/our-current-campaigns/pdsa-animal-wellbeing-report

Pet Business Insurance (2016) 'Pet Business Protection Policy'
http://www.petbusinessinsurance.co.uk/wp-content/uploads/2016/03/pet-business-protection-policy-
wording-march-2016.pdf

Pet Food Industry (2015) 'UK pet care spending to surpass US$7 billion in 2015'
http://www.petfoodindustry.com/articles/4858-uk-pet-care-spending-to-surpass-us-7-billion-in-2015

Petplan Sanctuary (2016) 'Policy Terms and Conditions'
https://www.petplansanctuary.co.uk/assets/pdf/PP-Sanc-16-TCs-7580-11.pdf

Portsmouth City Council (2011) 'Dog Control Orders Formal Notice'
https://www.portsmouth.gov.uk/ext/documents-external/cul-dco-formalnotice.pdf

Reading Borough Council (2015) 'Licence Conditions for Home Boarding of Dogs Overnight and
Day Creche'
http://www.reading.gov.uk/media/3695/Conditions-for-dog-home-boarding-
establishment/pdf/Conditions_for_dog_home_boarding_establishment__Aug_20153.pdf

RCVS (2016) 'Code of Professional Conduct for Veterinary Surgeons - Communication & Consent'
http://www.rcvs.org.uk/advice-and-guidance/code-of-professional-conduct-for-veterinary-
surgeons/supporting-guidance/communication-and-consent/

Scottish Natural Heritage (2013) 'Dog Owners - Scottish Outdoor Access Code'
http://www.snh.gov.uk/docs/A965891.pdf

Index

Advertise your home boarding business in the UK's biggest pet boarding directory:

Printed in Great Britain
by Amazon